Parental Alienation Syndrome in
Court Referred Custody Cases

by
Janelle Burrill-O'Donnell

ISBN: 1-58112-149-0

DISSERTATION.COM

USA • 2002

Parental Alienation Syndrome in Court Referred Custody Cases

Dissertation.com
USA • 2002

ISBN: 1-58112-149-0

www.dissertation.com/library/1121490a.htm

PARENTAL ALIENATION SYNDROME
IN COURT REFERRED CUSTODY CASES

A Dissertation

Presented to the Graduate Faculty of the College of Behavioral Sciences

Northcentral University

In Partial Fulfillment of the Requirements for the Degree

DOCTOR OF PHILOSOPHY

by

Janelle Burrill-O'Donnell

October 2001

APPROVAL

We, the undersigned, certify that we have read this dissertation and approve it as fully adequate in scope and quality for the degree of Doctor of Philosophy:

Author:　　Janelle Burrill-O'Donnell

Title:　　**Parental Alienation Syndrome in Court Referred Custody Cases**

Dissertation Committee:

_____　　_____

Chair:　G. Roy Sumpter, Ph.D.　　　　　　　　Date:

_____　　_____

Member:　Barbara Lackey, Ph.D.　　　　　　　Date:

_____　　_____

Member:　Gil Linne, Ph.D.　　　　　　　　　　Date:

ACKNOWLEDGMENTS

To my husband, John. Thank you for your support.

DISSERTATION ABSTRACT

Author: Janelle Burrill-O'Donnell, Ph.D.

Degree: Doctor of Philosophy

Institution: Northcentral University   Awarded: October, 2001

Title of Dissertation: **PARENTAL ALIENATION SYNDROME IN COURT REFERRED CUSTODY CASES**

Scope of Study: This dissertation summarizes the research of 30 court referred, custody dispute cases assessing the behaviors of the parents and their children to determine the presence or absence of Parental Alienation Syndrome (PAS). The criteria to determine the parent and their children's behaviors is Dr. Gardner's definition of Parental Alienation Syndrome. The parents were placed in three categories (mild, moderate or severe) based on their symptoms and behaviors. Their children (59) were then categorized into three groups (mild, moderate, severe). This investigation seeks to determine additional information regarding the presence or absence of PAS. Reluctance by the courts and mental health community to accept the validity of PAS probably contributes to the perpetuation of the disruption of parent-child relations in custody disputes.

Findings and Conclusions: It appears the data from this study corroborates observations and definitions of Parental Alienation Syndrome. The data from this study indicates that the parents in the mild PAS category have children who exhibit fewer negative behaviors toward the alienated parents whereas children whose parents are in the severe category exhibit more negative behaviors towards the alienated parents. This study found that the more negative behaviors a child exhibits towards an alienated parent, the more severe their parent's symptoms and behaviors. Consequently, there is more severe alienation from the alienated parent and the more disruption to that parent-child relation. PAS is a distinctive form of child abuse generally found in intractable custody disputes.

Chair Approval for Publication: Date:

iii

TABLE OF CONTENTS

Page

iv

LIST OF TABLES

ix

CHAPTER ONE
INTRODUCTION

The Parental Alienation Syndrome (PAS) so named by Dr. Richard Gardner, has been misinterpreted, misunderstood, and at times highly criticized. Legal, psychological, and psychiatric communities still "cringe" when PAS is suggested outright or is part of a court report. However, this researcher's professional clinical experience appears to support observations of PAS. This study will seek to determine the presence or absence of PAS in these 30 court referred cases.

Dr. Gardner is an experienced child and forensic psychiatrist who in 1985, introduced the concept of Parental Alienation Syndrome, and knew from experience that the norm for children of divorce was to continue to love and long for *both* parents and that children continue to long for both parents despite the passage of time subsequent to divorce (Rand, 1997; Dunne, 1994). "Parental Alienation Syndrome," is used to refer to a child's denigrating and rejecting a previously loved parent in the context of divorce or custody (Rand, 1997; Gardner, 1992).

In the early 1980's, there was concern in the mental health community about the increasing number of children who presented as preoccupied with denigrating one parent, even to the point of expressing hatred toward a once loved parent (Gardner, 1992; Rand, 1997). Dr. Gardner published his observations; however, his publication was from clinical observation only. Dr. Gardner is a practitioner seeking to improve the diagnostic skills and intervention strategies of the courts and other professionals who deal with high conflict custody cases (Rand, 1997). No specific research data is available to support clinical observations of PAS.

The purpose of this study is to determine whether there is support for observations of Parental Alienation Syndrome. A case study approach was used as the methodology. Gardner's criteria for PAS was used as the base for collecting data. Additionally, the signs and symptoms manifested by this study's participants (data collected) were defined using the Diagnostic and Statistical Manual of Mental Disorders, 4th ed. (APA, 1994).

PAS was explored and explained using Dr. Gardner's criteria which states in part: 1) the alienating parent's denigration of the alienated parent results in the child viewing that parent as loathsome, worthless and without any admirable qualities; 2) the child emulates the alienating parent; and 3) the child identifies with the alienating parent ("perfect parent") to the exclusion of the alienated parent.

This investigation analyzed thirty cases with 59 children currently in the court system to see if they support the existence of PAS. It examined the characteristics and behaviors of the alienating parents, the alienated parent, the child, as well as, the techniques used by the alienating parent, the responses of the child, and the responses of the alienated parent.

Reluctance by professionals to consider the existence of PAS contributes to the perpetuation of the alienation of children and destruction of a parent-child relation. It is believed by this researcher that an appropriate diagnosis of PAS can make the difference between allowing the case to go beyond the point of no return or intervening effectively before it is too late to save the parent-child relationship and maintain the emotional stability of children.

Manifestations of and Definitions of Parental Alienation Syndrome

Syndrome

A syndrome is defined as a grouping of signs and symptoms, based upon their frequent occurrence that may suggest a common underlying pathogenesis, course, familial pattern, or treatment selection (DSM 4th Edition, 1994). The syndrome identified by Gardner seeks to understand the process of a child aligning with one parent against the other parent in a legal context.

PAS was first observed in children who had been involved in protracted custody litigation. Parental alienation is now so common that manifestations of PAS were observed in approximately 90% of the children involved in custody conflicts by the mid 1980's (Gardner, 1992).

PAS vs. Brainwashing

PAS is different from simple brainwashing, and the term PAS refers to a "disturbance in which a child is preoccupied with denigration and criticism of a parent." (Gardner, 1992). The criticism and denigration of PAS is unjustified and/or exaggerated. Gardner stated, "Brainwashing implies one parent is systematically and consciously programming the child to denigrate the other" (Gardner, 1992, p. 64.). While the concept of PAS includes the brainwashing component, it is much more comprehensive. PAS includes not only conscious coercion, but "unconscious factors within the programming parent" which contribute to the child's alienation from the alienated parent (Gardner, 1992; 1998; 1999).

PAS emphasizes factors that arise within the child which are independent of the parental contributions that initiated the development of PAS. Clinical observations emphasized the combination of the child's own scenarios of denigration of the alienated parent and the alienating parent's programming. PAS is a term, which includes and encompasses <u>both</u> contributory factors of the child and the alienating parent.

PAS is not animosity that a child harbors against a parent who has actually abused that child. PAS will not be considered if the parent is found neglectful and/or abusive. In such cases, it is appropriate for the child to want to cease contact with the abusing parent. "PAS is applicable only when the [alienated] parent has not exhibited anything close to the degree of alienating behavior that might warrant the campaign of denigration exhibited by the child" (Gardner, 1992, p. 64). Rather, in typical cases, the alienated parent would be considered by most evaluators to have been a normal, loving parent or at worst, exhibited "minimal impairments in parenting capacity" (Gardner, 1992, p. 64; 1998; 1999). It is the exaggerating of minor weaknesses and deficiencies by a child that is the hallmark of PAS.

<u>The Children</u>

When bona fide abuse is present, the PAS diagnosis is not applicable. No single child is going to exhibit all of the symptoms of PAS; rather, the symptoms can be divided into mild, moderate, and severe categories. For example, the severely alienated child is obsessed with "hatred of a parent" (Gardner, 1992, p. 64). The denigration of the parent often has the quality of a litany: "I hate him and I never want to see him again" because "he scares me." The once revered parent is now referred to as "boring" and "mean". The child has no memory of any happy, good, or positive times prior to the alienated parent's departure.

The relationship between the alienated parent and child is fragile in these families even if it was positive <u>prior</u> to the separation. Children have a diminished ability to maintain healthy boundaries and relationships when brought into conflict in a custody battle.

Dr. Stahl (1999) suggests children are most susceptible to alienation when they are passive and dependent and feel a strong need to psychologically care for the alienating parent. In both the child and the alienating parent, there is a sense of moral outrage at the alienated parent and there is typically a fusion of feelings between the alienating parent and child such that they talk about the alienated parent as having hurt "us" (Stahl, P., 1999, p. 4). Dr. Stahl believes the children in such families are likely to develop a variety of pathological symptoms which can include: 1) splitting in their relationships; 2) difficulties in forming intimate relationships; 3) a lack of ability to tolerate anger in other relationships; 4) psychosomatic symptoms; 5) conflicts with authority figures; and 6) an unhealthy sense of entitlement that leads to social alienation in general.

It is important for the evaluator to make an attempt to divide children with manifestations of PAS into mild, moderate, and severe categories. As is true of all psychiatric disorders, there is a continuum from the mildest through the moderate, to the most severe.

Mild PAS

The children in this category may develop their own scenarios about the alienated parent with only slight prodding by the alienating parent. Here, the children's primary motive is to strengthen the alienating parent's position in the custody dispute in order to maintain the psychological bond they have with that parent. These children present as ambivalent about visitation, but are the most free to express affection for the alienated parent even in the alienating parent's presence.

Moderate PAS

The children in this category are less fanatic in their vilification of the alienated parent than those children in the severe category. However, these children do have campaigns of deprecation of the alienated parent, but are much more "likely to give up their own scenarios" when alone with the alienated parent, especially for long periods. When these children are removed entirely from the alienating parent's purview, they quiet down, relax, and involve themselves with the alienated parent. The primary motive of the child's scenario is to maintain the psychological bond with the alienating parent.

Severe PAS

These children are easy to recognize. When the therapist or evaluator invites everyone for a family interview or for an interview of the children with each parent separately, the alienating parent was sitting on one side of the waiting room with the children acting as if the alienated parent was not present in the waiting room. Typically, the child sits next to the alienating parent, who tries to find a position most remote from the alienated parent. "The professions of hatred are most intense when the child and the alienating parent are in the presence of the alienated parent." (Gardner, 1992; 1998; 1999).

However, when the child is alone with the alienated parent, he or she may exhibit feelings, which range from: 1) hatred, 2) neutrality, or 3) inhibited expressions of affection. Children provide the most frivolous excuses for not visiting which are supported by the alienating parent. Visitation is strongly resisted by these children. In pre-adolescents and adolescents, visitation frequently stops.

Manifestations of the Alienating Parent in PAS

It is not unusual for one to see a family in which the allegiance of the children has been "split." One or more children may side with the mother and one or more children may side with the father. However, it is the introduction of the children's *own* scenarios, which warrant the PAS designation. The alienating parent desires to maintain a strong psychological bond with the child. "Obviously, the custody dispute threatens this bond and there is the omnipresent risk of its interruption, attenuation and possibly even its ultimate obliteration." (Gardner, 1992, p. 121.)

Parents with Mild PAS

The alienating parents with mild PAS are healthy enough not to involve themselves in courtroom litigation in order to gain primary custody. These parents recognize that alienation from the other parent is not in the best interests of their child and make a more conciliatory approach to the alienated parent's request. However, some manifestations of programming are visible in the alienating parent in order to strengthen their position. "There is no paranoia here, but there is anger and there may be some desire for vengeance" ...These parents are typically entrenched in their positions and feel they are in an unequal situation with the other parent" (Gardner, 1992, p. 154).

Parents with Moderate PAS

This is about the parent, not the child. These parent's exhibit rage and paranoia in severe cases. Their rage may stem from feelings of abandonment by the other parent (Roseby, 1993; 1998).

These parents are able to differentiate between sexual/physical abuse allegations that are preposterous and those that are not. Nonetheless, there is still a campaign of denigration and a significant desire to withhold the child from the other parent as a vengeance maneuver. These parents will find a variety of excuses to interfere with or circumvent visitation. These parents may be unreceptive to complying with court orders; however, they will often comply with threats of sanctions or transfer of custody.

For example, when a sex abuse allegation occurs, these parents are able to differentiate between the child's obviously "coached" claims of abuse and those that may have validity. The parents in this category are more likely to have been good child-rearers prior to the separation/divorce. In contrast, the parents in the severe category had serious impairments in child rearing capacity prior to the separation/divorce.

Parents with Severe PAS

The alienating parent in PAS, severe type, often manifest psychopathic elements. Their maneuvers may be sadistic in an attempt to totally eliminate the alienated parent. According to Gardner, (1992; 1998; 1999) the (severe) alienating parent's "cruel maneuvers are often derivatives of psychopathological processes that become incorporated" into the alienating parent's programming resulting in exclusionary procedures of the alienated parent.

In severe PAS, these parents are often fanatics. They will frequently use every mechanism at their disposal (legal and illegal) to prevent and interrupt visitation with the alienated parent. The alienating parents are obsessed with antagonism and anger toward the other parent. "In many cases they are paranoid" (Gardner, 1992, p. 150).

Frequently, the paranoia that becomes so apparent did not exhibit itself prior to the breakup of the relationship or marriage, but may now be the manifestation of the psychiatric deterioration seen in the context of custody/divorce disputes (Gardner, 1985; 1992). "Central to the paranoid mechanism is projection" (Gardner, 1992, p. 150). The alienating parent sees the other parent as having many noxious qualities, which actually exist within themselves. These alienating parents project these unacceptable qualities onto the other parent so they can consider themselves innocent victims.

Alienating parents in severe PAS cases do not respond to logic, confrontations with reality or appeals to reason. They truly believe their preposterous scenarios. It takes skilled mental health examiners to maintain a therapeutic relationship with the entire family. Frequently, there is no evidence for the alienating parent's accusations. This includes even a court decision that the alienated parent is not guilty of the allegations made by the alienating parent. The child in severe PAS joins and shares in the paranoid fantasies about the alienated parent with the alienating parent. These children may become panic-stricken over the prospect of visiting the other parent. Visitation frequently becomes impossible.

Internal Processes Involved in Alienating

The below definitions and examples may help the reader understand the alienating parents' internal processes.

Reaction Formation

Reaction formation is an unconscious process whereby an individual controls what he or she believes to be unacceptable feelings or impulses by establishing behavior patterns, which are directly opposed to the unacceptable feelings, or impulses. Even though the original impulse is repressed, it is believed to continue to exist unconsciously in its original form and is thus, "likely to emerge under some circumstances" (Reber, 1995). An alienating parent may cover his or her feelings about the other parent and use anger as the mechanism to cover up affection. It is very important to understand that many alienating parents may not be loving toward the child, but rather may ostensibly campaign against the other parent in their so-called attempt to "protect the child from harm by the alienated parent" (Gardner, 1992).

A healthy parent, a parent who truly loves his/her child, appreciates the importance of the noncustodial parent in the life of their child and, with the exception of the genuinely abusing parent, facilitate meaningful contact between the child and their former spouse. Parental deficiency is a manifestation of PAS and is not in the child's best interests. The alienating parent's apparent obsessive love of their child may often be an attempt to cover up their underlying hostility (Lund, J., Sullivan, M., 1996).

Projection

The mechanism of projection is often operative for many of the alienating parents, particularly the moderate and severe category. (Rand, 1997). Projection is an unconscious process by which a person's own traits, emotions, or dispositions are ascribed to another. Frequently, there is denial that these feelings or tendencies exist. Projection functions as a defense mechanism to protect the alienating parent from the underlying conflict and feelings that have been repressed (Reber, 1995).

The alienating parent attributes to the other parent tendencies and practices, which are unlikely, if not impossible, and are products of their own imaginations. The alienating parent can then consider him or herself free of odious behavior (Gardner, 1992; 1998). For example, an alienating parent attributes inappropriate touching of a child to the alienated parent. The child can come to believe this distortion of reality and fear the alienated parent.

Mental health professionals believe the alienating parent may be able to correct the distorted thinking by logic and confrontation with reality. However, if this does not occur and the belief becomes fixed and unswerving in spite of confrontation, "then the term paranoid is well warranted" (Gardner, 1992, p. 126).

Many accusations are conscious and deliberate; however, in other cases subconscious and unconscious factors are operative, especially projection. This is primarily observed in PAS, severe type. For example, an alienating parent's own suppressed and repressed sexual fantasies are projected onto the child and the other parent. There may be accusations of sexual abuse, physical abuse, and/or domestic violence without evidence.

Paranoia

A disorder manifesting suspiciousness of delusional proportions typical of this disorder or the belief of some harm to self or another exists (DSM 4th Ed., 1994). In PAS, paranoia is expressed by obsession with antagonism toward the other parent. Sometimes the paranoid thoughts and feelings about the other parent are isolated to that person alone; however, in other cases this paranoia is just one example of many types of paranoid thinking in the alienating parent (Gardner, 1992). For example, a parent may have paranoid delusions that the other parent is seeking to take the child away when in fact the other parent just wants a consistent parenting schedule and an opportunity to share the parenting. The paranoid belief system is also transferred to the children by instilling fear that the other parent is attempting to take the child away. For example, a child will express (during an interview) that "he doesn't want anymore time with his father because his father is mean and he is trying to hurt my mother by taking me away from her." There is no evidence to support these fears and beliefs, which the mother has projected onto the child.

Anger

Anger is used to describe the alienating parent's behavior towards the alienated parent. The anger fuels the campaign of denigration and the desire to withhold the child from the alienated parent as a vengeance maneuver. Anger in alienating parents is also exhibited by finding a wide variety of excuses to interfere with or circumvent visitation with the alienated parent. Psychodynamically, angry or raging parents may feel abandoned by the other parent. In their rage and anger they pull the child toward them in an attempt to not feel abandoned by the child, and they begin a campaign of deprecation against the child's other parent. The anger fuels this campaign for years until appropriate intervention by the courts and mental health professionals is in place (Rand, 1997).

Programming the Child

Programming is defined as a parent who denigrates and criticizes the alienated parent overtly and covertly. For example, "I can't afford to send you to private school anymore because your father left us and won't pay child support." These kinds of statements are frequently said in a variety of ways and situations, but the message is always the same: "your father did this to us." This is but one example of many different kinds of statements made repeatedly to program a child.

Allegations of Sexual Abuse or Physical Abuse

Allegations of sex abuse or physical abuse frequently occur often resulting in long periods without contact between the child and the alienated parent. An investigation must take place and the parent is typically on supervised visitation pending the outcome of the investigation. For example, a child may state to the mental health professional, "My Daddy touched my privates." During the investigation, authorities found this child had no idea what her "privates" meant; she was two and one-half years old. However, a four-year-old boy stated over and over his father put his "fingers in his bottom and rolled him in a sheet." In both cases, the alleged abuse was not substantiated. However, the alienating parent's belief that the abuse occurred was not altered; and the allegations and discussions continued until the children were removed from the alienating parent's custody.

Compliance with Court Orders

Generally, mild alienating parents will not only comply with court orders, they will follow the court orders. However, moderately alienating parents will often comply with a court order only if there is a threat of contempt or modification of a current parenting schedule. Severe alienating parents will not comply with court orders, or even the threat of modification of custody, including a reversal of custody or the threat of contempt.

For example, a mother of two preadolescent daughters had refused to transfer the minors for even supervised visitation with the Father. The minors' resistance to visitation with the father increased. A reversal of custody to father was ordered by the court. The minors resided with father with court ordered supervised visitation with their mother. The mother stopped contact with the minors.

Overprotective Parents

Parental overprotection and PAS can overlap. An overprotective parent communicates to the child this message: "The world is a dangerous place and calamity may befall you at anytime. Stick by my side and I will protect you from these catastrophes" (Gardner, 1992, p. 129). Overprotection can result in fear and anxiety in the child, but does not result in fear of and hatred of that child's other parent unless PAS is present.

Gardner (1992, p. 122; 1985) states, "One factor operative in maternal overprotection is anger." Another operative factor in the development of overprotection is the parent's need for gratification of their own infantile dependency needs. Additionally, overprotection of a child can serve to compensate for feelings of low self-worth. The alienating parent comes to view himself or herself as a "super parent." An overprotective parent is a "high risk candidate for providing the kind of programming that may result in a parental alienation syndrome" (Gardner, 1992, p. 131).

Preexisting anxieties and phobias can become intensified at the time of separation which exacerbate the alienating parent's need for the child's companionship and even protection by the child.

Alienated Parent

Frequently, the alienated parent is passive, dismayed, and befuddled. The alienated parent is in the midst of the PAS process before he or she begins to recognize there is a serious problem in their parent-child relationship. In mild to moderate PAS, behavior of the alienated parent may contribute significantly to the PAS process. "Blush and Ross observed that falsely accused fathers tended to display passive or dependent features as compared with their more histrionic spouses" (Rand, 1997, p. 57). However, in severe PAS, the alienated parent may be relatively healthy and contribute minimally to the PAS, compared to the alienating parent (Rand, 1997).

Conclusion

PAS remains distinctive to intractable conflict in divorce and/or custody disputes in which the child becomes aligned with one parent and preoccupied with unjustified and/or exaggerated denigration of the alienated parent. Detection of PAS and an understanding of appropriate remedial treatments to restore the child's relationship with the alienated parent has not occurred (Rand, 1997).

Brief Overview of Related Literature

Described here is a brief overview of related literature which is warranted to understand the history, development, and symptomology of PAS. Since the publication of Dr. Gardner's 1985 article on *Parental Alienation Syndrome*, he has continued to expand his understanding of the ideology, development, manifestations and treatment of this disorder which is often seen in the context of child custody disputes. According to Gardner, (1992) he began observing children whom he considered "brainwashed by one parent" in the early 1980's. Since that time, the incidence of PAS has increased. PAS is typically seen in children who have been involved in protracted custody litigation.

Children may tell very moving stories about how they have not liked or been fearful of the alienated parent for a long time (Stahl, 1999). Stahl reports there may have been an absence of a quality relationship in the formative years of development of the child and the alienated parent. There may exist a superficiality to the parent-child relationship so that the alienating parent was truly the "primary parent" in the marital relationship (Stahl, 1999). The alienated parent may show up for the "Kodak moments," but probably do so in a more self-centered way, often for his or her own enjoyment, rather than to participate with his or his child.

However, there are limitations to Dr. Gardner's reports. He relies solely on his own clinical observations. His reports have not undergone the scrutiny of any studies by mental health professionals with access to his reported data.

Methodology

This study will review the 30 court referred cases to determine the presence or absence of criteria for PAS. The differences between the three categories (i.e. mild, moderate, and severe) were compared using the criteria for the children's behaviors and parental behaviors. The criteria used to evaluate the data is set out in Chapter 3.

The thirty cases used in this study were either court referred to this researcher for evaluation, mediation, or therapy. These cases were chosen on the basis of intractable parental conflict and custody dispute. There is no attempt to match these cases with a control group.

Descriptive statistics were used to describe this study's observations. Measures of variability in the categories for children's symptoms and parents' symptoms using PAS criteria was described. The data obtained from the thirty case sample will describe parents using the parental criteria for PAS: mild, moderate and severe. Data from the criteria of the children's symptoms with PAS (mild, moderate, and severe) were reviewed.

What a parent says to his or her child and a parent's behavior affects the child's feelings and behavior towards the other parent. This study reviewed cases in the mild, moderate, and severe parental PAS categories. The criteria used to categorize these cases was Gardner's criteria based on the <u>parents' symptoms.</u>

The children in each case were compared in one of the three (mild, moderate, severe) categories based upon Gardner's criteria for the <u>child's symptoms</u>. The children were compared in each separate category to see what was found. The child's symptoms in each case in each category (mild, moderate, severe) were compared to see if they differ in symptomology between the three groups. Nonparametric statistics, one-way analysis of covariance was used here.

Demographic data obtained for both the parents and the children consists of gender, age, and race. Nonparametric statistics is used here. If the data for the parents is sound and results from the children's data supports the PAS criteria, then Gardner's observations and findings are sound.

The research questions are: 1) Can observations of Parental Alienation Syndrome be supported; and 2) What, if any difference exists between the three groups of children in this study?

The symptomology criteria used is Gardner's PAS for both the parents and children (Appendix C, D). In order to replicate this study, the researcher needs access to court cases that include interviews of mother and father conjointly and individually, and conjoint interviews with each parent and minors and each minor individually. (Appendix A, B).

The information letter (Appendix E) was sent to all persons informing them of the study and that the data from their records was included in this study. Confidentiality was maintained at all times. This researcher will not have contact with subjects, only the data contained in their files.

Limitations of this Study

Gathering and reviewing data about an individual or individuals is a way of studying a broader phenomenon. The general purpose of this study was to identify intractable, custody disputes in which the PAS criteria was used in order to determine whether the existence of PAS can be supported. The criteria for PAS was used to determine whether these types of cases in a custody context can support mental health professionals' observations of PAS.

However, there are limitations to this study. More specifically, to assume this small sample (n=30) can be generalized necessitates assumption that the sample is representative of PAS in intractable custody disputes. However, if the alternative hypothesis is correct, then mental health professionals and the courts can generalize to other intractable, high conflict custody cases which also meet the criteria for PAS. Since only intractable, custody dispute cases are examined, this creates a restriction of the range of the cases analyzed.

Research Expectations

Accurate recognition, diagnosis, and proper treatment of Parental Alienation Syndrome may prevent further deterioration and rupture of the alienated parent-child relationship. In order to move forward with support from the courts, judges, lawyers, and mental health community, it is important that there is support for the validity of Parental Alienation Syndrome's existence. Delays in diagnosis and treatment can compromise the best interests of the child.

CHAPTER TWO

REVIEW OF RELATED LITERATURE

Background

Historically, for over 300 years the adversary system has developed to include

the court's rules of procedure, evidence, and lawyer ethics. The traditional adversarial

courtroom conflict has its attorneys, clients, and witnesses. Attorneys and their clients

get swept up in courtroom battles, and the only goal is to win. The adversary system,

which professes to help parents resolve their differences today, may intensify the

hostilities between the parents rather than reducing the conflict.

Litigation of parental rights now contributes to an ever-increasing vicious cycle

of vengeance which stretches even beyond the grievances of the marriage or relationship

prior to court. Some attorneys appreciate the terrible psychological trauma that

frequently results from protracted adversarial proceedings, other attorneys do not.

Venting anger tends to "feed on itself" (Rand 1997; Gardner, 1992).

There are many parents who, at the time of separation, "make serious attempts to

avoid psychologically debilitating litigation" (Gardner, 1992, p. 43). These parents wish

to avoid unnecessary and traumatic experiences for themselves and their child. While

the adversary system may not be necessarily detrimental in other areas of the law,

custody and divorce can lead to protracted custody litigation with a "high risk of a wide

variety of psychopathological reactions" by the parents (Gardner, 1992, p. 51; 1998).

Prior to the 1920's, custody of minor children was automatically given to fathers.

However, the "tender-years presumption" presumed mothers were intrinsically

19

preferable to fathers as child rearers "unless a father could prove the mother grossly unfit" (Gardner, 1992, p. 51; 1998). In other words, the judge must *presume* that the mother is the preferable parent. The divorce rate was relatively low until the mid 1940's; however, since World War II, there has been a "progressive increase in the divorce rate" as well as an increase in custody litigation.

Divorce laws in most states were predicated on concepts of guilt and innocence within the context of punishment and restitution. Divorce was granted when the petitioner proved he or she had been "wronged or injured" by the respondent.

In the 1960's, the traditional grounds for divorce were no longer viewed as simply a "wrong perpetrated by one party," but that "both parties" contributed to the marital breakdown (Rand, 1997). Statutes were passed in the states and were referred to as "no fault divorce laws." The basis to grant a divorce was that of "incompatibility." Now the notion that a woman is automatically a preferable parent was claimed a "sexist concept" by fathers. New statutes were soon passed which clearly stated the sex of a parent will not be a consideration when settling a custody dispute. The tender years presumption was replaced with the "*best interests-of-the-child-presumption*" (Gardner, 1992; 1998; Rand, 1997). Fathers now had a chance to gain custody; the custody battles began. Since the mid 1970's children have become "open territory" in child custody conflicts.

Joint Custody

By the late 1970's and early 1980's joint custody gained in popularity. Rather than one parent designated as the sole custodial parent and the other parent just a "visitor," it was now considered possible that both parents could "share" in the parenting of their child. Ideally, for the joint custodial concept to work, both parents must be able to communicate and cooperate well with each other and to be equally capable of assuming child-rearing responsibilities. The parents' living situation must be one of which they can both participate in taking the children to and from school, extracurricular activities and agree cooperatively what those activities are to be.

The main drawback of granting joint custody, frequently and automatically, is that the children may be used as pawns in the parental conflicts. Such use of children is likely because there are no restraints placed on non-cooperating parents and conflict becomes continuous.

Sole Custody

The sole custodial arrangement does not protect children entirely from being used as pawns, but it does reduce the opportunities for parents to involve their children in such manipulations. Joint custody requires an in depth assessment of the parents' parenting capacities, cooperation, shared parenting potential, and psychological status.

Parents who resort to litigating for custody, particularly if it is repetitive litigation, are typically not capable of cooperating with one another, and in most cases, are not communicating well either (Rand, 1997). Yet, the Family Law Relations Court is a system which may be one of the poorest yet devised to help to investigate and deal with parental conflicts and disputes. Many forms of psychopathology result from the utilization of the system as a method for resolving custody conflicts. Parental Alienation Syndrome (PAS), one of the most common forms of "psychiatric disorders" that results from the attempt to deal with divorce and custody disputes may be a result of the adversary system (Gardner, 1985; 1989; 1992).

Parental Alienation Syndrome

PAS is a relatively recent disorder, having evolved from recent changes in the criteria by which primary custodial placement is decided. Beginning in the 1970's, courts have taken the position that the "tender years presumption" is sexist and that custodial determinations should be made on criteria relating directly to parenting capacity, independent of gender.

Now, a law protects the child by the "best interests" of the child standard typically granting joint custody and joint decision-making powers to the parents. This has the effect of making children's custodial arrangements more predictable and also more precarious. As a result, programming children by parents to ensure "victory" in the custody/visitation litigation is common. Gardner (1992) believes 90% of all custody evaluations involve Parental Alienation Syndrome.

The Parental Alienation Syndrome so named by Dr. Richard Gardner has been misinterpreted, misunderstood and highly criticized (Gardner, 1992; Rand, 1997). By the 1980's, he began to observe a disorder rarely seen previously. Gardner (1985) described the syndrome as arising primarily in children who have been involved in protracted custody litigation. For example, the alienating parent may make accusations about the alienated parent in front of the child and may tell the child the alienated parent does not love him or her.

PAS is referred to as a disturbance in which children are preoccupied with deprecation and criticism of a parent, including denigration which is unjustified and exaggerated. Children are not merely brainwashed, although the brainwashing component is part of PAS (Gardner, 1985; 1992; Nicholas, 1996). However, the alienating parent uses conscious, as well as unconscious, factors to program the child and alienate him or her from the other (alienated) parent.

PAS includes factors that arise within the child. These factors are independent of the parental contributions although the child's behavior probably would not arise in the first place without contribution by the programming parent (Gardner, 1992; Rand, 1997). Consequently, PAS is combined with the child's own scenarios of denigration along with the programming parent's contribution. Situational factors may contribute i.e., factors which exist within a family either prior to the separation or as a result of the separation.

PAS is never used to describe the animosity a child may display against a parent who has actually abused that child, especially over an extended period of time. PAS is applicable only when the "alienated parent has not exhibited anything close to the degree of alienating behavior which might warrant the campaign of denigration exhibited by the child" (Gardner, 1992, p. 60). Rather, it is the exaggeration of minor weaknesses and deficiencies that is the hallmark of the PAS (Gardner, 1992). The child resists contact with the alienated parent.

Manifestations of PAS in Parents

PAS is the syndrome described in 1985 for the phenomenon observed wherein a child from a "broken home" becomes alienated from one parent due to the active efforts of the other parent to sever the parent-child relationship. In PAS, the child becomes aware that the alienating parent wants him or her to hate the other parent and, out of a strong need to please the alienating parent and avoid abandonment or rejection, the child joins in the denigration of the alienated parent (Siegle, J., & Langford, J., 1998).

Gardner (1992) and Clawar and Rivlin (1991) have described numerous behaviors the alienating parent may engage in to harm the child's relationship with the alienated parent. Gardner describes the child as being "programmed" rather than brainwashed. The alienating parent may make accusations about the alienated parent in front of the child. For example, the alienated parent may be described as dangerous or harmful, and the alienated parent's faults (real or imagined) are often exaggerated. (Siegel, J., and Langford, J., 1998).

Rand (1997) indicates there is an increasing number of theoretical writings, case studies, and anecdotal accounts related to this phenomena which have now begun to appear in the literature. Some researchers and clinicians use the term PAS while others use different terminology. Many questions remain unanswered about PAS. However, the purpose of this study is to investigate and examine thirty court referred cases currently in the court system and to provide data which may or may not support the existence of PAS. Reluctance by professionals to consider the existence of PAS may contribute to the perpetuation of the alienation of children and the loss of parent-child relationships.

<u>The Parents in PAS</u>

Mild PAS Symptoms in Parents

The alienating parent in mild PAS is healthy enough not to involve themselves in significant degrees of courtroom litigation in order to gain primary custody. These parents recognize the other parent as important in their child's life. However, some manifestations of programming are visible by the alienating parent in order to strengthen their position. "There is no paranoia here, but there is anger and there may be some desire for vengeance" (Gardner, 1992, p. 154). Of the three categories of alienating parents, these parents have generally been the most dedicated during the earliest years of their children's lives and have thereby developed the strongest and healthiest psychological bonds with them.

Moderate PAS Symptoms in Parents

These parents may present with more rage rather than paranoia which is more commonly observed in severe PAS. These parents can distinguish between sex abuse allegations that are preposterous and those that are not. However, these parents may denigrate and have a significant desire to withhold the child from the alienated parent as a "vengeance maneuver" (Gardner, 1992). These parents will find a variety of excuses to interfere with or circumvent visitation. These parents probably have a healthy psychological bond with the child that is being compromised by their rage (Gardner, 1992; 1998; Rand, 1997).

Severe PAS Symptoms in Parents

These parents often manifest psychopathic elements which are incorporated into their maneuvers in an attempt to eliminate the alienated parent. In severe PAS, these parents are often fanatics, and will use "every mechanism (legal and illegal) to prevent visitation" with the alienated parent. The alienating parents are obsessed with anger towards the other parent (Rand, 1997). "In many cases they are paranoid" (Gardner, 1992, p. 150).

Alienating parents in severe PAS cases do not respond to logic, confrontations with reality, or appeals to reason (Rand, 1997). These parents truly believe their preposterous scenarios. These parents frequently act in a histrionic manner at the time of exchange of the child; they make intrusive phone calls to the child while the child is visiting the alienated parent, and portray the alienated parent as harmful or dangerous to the child (Nicholas, L., 1995, unpublished).

The alienating parent may seek out a therapist to support collusive relationships, often without the alienated parent's knowledge or consent. Typically, the alienating parent attempts to manipulate the therapist to intercede by halting visitation with the alienated parent (Nicholas, 1995). False allegations of sexual or other abuse may be lodged against the alienated parent. These sex-abuse allegations frequently stop visitation. These parents have very poor boundaries between the parent and child. Programming of the child occurs. For example, the alienating parent uses the word "us" instead of "me" as in "he did this to 'us' in court" or "we don't trust him." This disrupts the child's psychological bond with the alienated parent (Gardner, 1992; 1998; Rand, 1997).

It is difficult to subdivide parents into meaningful categories. Such difficulty is a testament to the versatility and creativity of the parents who have devised the maneuvers in which they program their child. Almost any excuse known to humanity can be utilized to justify obstructing the parenting plan and visitation schedule. There is no detail on which to focus with regard to alienating and disrupting the parent-child relationship; the PAS process is complex.

The alienating parent desires maintenance of the primary psychological bond with the child. Custody disputes weaken and threaten this bond. Nonetheless, there are certainly many other factors which contribute to programming a child in order to produce PAS. Preexisting anxieties, anger, phobias, substance abuse, deprivations in the parent's childhood, death of a parent and depression are a few of the factors which could contribute to PAS (Gardner, 1992).

Psychological Factors Which Drive the Alienating Parent

The alienating parent frequently feels abandonment and rage, and desires revenge. This parent harbors old wounds from the failed relationship. The alienating parent may have predisposing mental or emotional impairments (Gardner, 1992; 1998). Often the alienating parent has an excessively dependent relationship with the child and may be overprotective (Gardner, 1992; Nicholas, 1995). The alienating parent's investment in the alienation process is related to his or her own feelings and needs, not the child's needs. The alienating parent desires to maintain a strong psychological bond with the child.

It is not unusual to see a family in which the allegiance of the children has been "split." One or more child may side with the mother and one or more child may side with the father. Each child may reside primarily with a different parent.

Clawar and Rivlin (1991) report alienating parents present with "self-righteousness" as an important motivation to program the child. According to Blush and Ross (1987) mothers tend to be histrionic in presentation and emotionally convinced of the "facts" that no amount of input, including that from neutral professionals, can sway them from their perceptions. Blush and Ross (1987) indicate the typical profile for alienating fathers is one of intellectual rigidity and a high need to be "correct."

Rogers (1992) reported five divorce/custody cases in which the falsely accusing parent suffered from delusional disorder. The children in Rogers (1992) study were all subjected to undue influence to get them to accept the accusing parents' psychotic belief and concomitant rejection of the alienated parent in severe PAS scenarios. The five cases had subtle signs of suspiciousness during the marriage; however, during custody litigation there was noticeable deterioration in the alienating parent's parenting capabilities. Four out of the five cases resulted in the alienated parent eventually obtaining custody of the children (Rogers, 1992; Rand, 1997).

Wallerstein and Kelly (1980) wrote that alignment with one parent is a response of the "youngsters'" and is a reaction to the dramatic change in the relationship between parents and children. These children were vulnerable to being swept up in the anger of one parent against the other. Not infrequently, they turned on the parent they had loved and been very close to prior to the separation. The most extreme identification with the parental cause is called "alignment" - a divorce specific relationship which occurs "when a parent and one or more children join in a vigorous attack on the other parent" (Wallerstein and Kelly, 1980). Wallerstein and Kelly (1980) noted nearly twice as many children united with their mothers as with their fathers.

Wallerstein and Kelly (1980) found the most useful allies in the divorce-related fighting were the nine-to-twelve-year-old boys and girls. A child at this age has the capacity to be an unswervingly loyal friend or team member. Mothers do better at courting their sons as allies, and fathers succeeded better with their daughters (Wallerstein and Kelly, 1980). The life span of these alignments appears to be related to custodial arrangement.

For example, Wallerstein and Kelly (1980) found that alignments with the alienated father (noncustodial parent) do not appear to last past the first post-separation year. Only a very few children continued in an alignment beyond that time. Almost all of these children had a failed separation-individuation from their mothers prior to the separation. On the other hand, maternal alignments, or alignments with the custodial parent, remain stable at the first year and one-half after separation.

Parents who maintained alignments after the first year were disturbed and angry people. These parents used anger to ward off pending depressions. Thus, this could explain the intensity of their anger which remained undiminished for a long time after separation (Wallerstein and Kelly, 1980).

Programming the Child

Programming a child is a set of instructions to sever the alienated parent-child relationship. However, brainwashing is the conscious denial of the existence of the alienated parent (Kelly, 1999). For example, the alienating parent turns away from the alienated parent in front of the child; or makes statements such as "Dad has a new car and we can't even afford pizza; do you think it's fair?" The threat of withdrawal of the alienating parent's love is involved as a factor in the programming. The child knows the alienating parent is fragile. Unfortunately, for these children some of these parents "rewrite reality" daily.

Kelly (1999) believes these alienating parents are motivated by revenge, self-entitlement, ownership, jealousy, loss of identity as the primary parent and psychopathology. For example, the custody dispute may be an organizing factor giving the alienating parent an identity wherein they look less "flaky."

Dr. Gardner (1985; 1992) believes his syndrome is different from simple brainwashing and describes PAS as a "disturbance in which a child is preoccupied with denigration and criticism of a parent." Gardner stated, "brainwashing is where one parent systematically and consciously programs the child to denigrate the other parent" (Gardner, 1992, p. 64). Gardner (1992) believes PAS includes the brainwashing component, but is much more comprehensive. Kelly (1999) stated, "programming is a set of specific instructions" to sever the alienated parent-child relationship. It would appear Kelly believes brainwashing exists outside the PAS spectrum. On the other hand, Gardner maintains PAS includes brainwashing, but combines conscious as well as *unconscious* factors of the alienating parent (Gardner, 1992).

The Child in PAS

Children of divorce/custody desire an ongoing relationship with both parents. In fact, a majority of children are eager to visit their noncustodial parents (Wallerstein and Kelly, 1980). Children long for both parents. Children in alignments are found to be less psychologically healthy than those whose custody/divorce allowed them to maintain their affection for both parents (Rand, 1997). Lampel (1997) found aligned children, less well adjusted and less able to conceptualize complex situations.

Lampel (1997) found that children's lack of normal ambivalence noteworthy in seven cases. This symptom corresponds with observations that alienated children respond with diminished or no ambivalence towards the alienated parent, particularly in moderate and severe PAS.

Children who refuse to visit is a surprising, perplexing and serious problem, yet it has received so little "systematic attention by researchers" (Johnston, 1993). Johnston's research lead to the conclusion that children's resistance or refusal to visit the noncustodial parent after separation is an overt behavioral symptom which has its roots in multiple, interlocking psychological, developmental and family systemic processes (Rand, 1997; Johnston, 1993; Clawar and Rivlin 1991).

Children three to six years old in high conflict divorce tend to shift their allegiances depending on which parent they are with (Johnston, 1993). This may result in problems with exchanges from one home to another. Children in this age group have not yet learned to entertain two conflicting points of view. For example, when a child is told by father that mother does not cook enough food, the child will align with father. The child will then shift allegiance to mother when told that father just wastes food. Children in this age group become easily confused and can readily excite concern and chaos by telling different stories to each parent. Children in this age group shift their preferences back and forth from one parent to the other, as they grow older and sort out their gender identity (Johnston, 1993).

Children of divorce/custody in the six to seven year age range are more likely to suffer from loyalty conflicts. Children seven to nine years of age have now developed the capacity to imagine how their parents view the other parent and experience cognitive dissonance because of their parents' conflicting views (Rand, 1997; Johnston, 1993).

Children in the nine to twelve year age group are particularly vulnerable to forming strong, PAS alignments with one parent, as they try to "resolve their earlier loyalty conflicts" (Rand, 1997, p. 44; Johnston, 1993). The children in this age group were from high conflict divorced families. Johnston indicated the figures "approach Gardner's estimate that 90% of the children he has assessed in custody evaluations exhibit varying degrees of PAS" (Rand, 1997; Johnston, 1993).

Sometimes, teenagers develop the capacity to take a more objective, independent stance and no longer engage in the PAS process. However, a significant proportion of "high conflict divorce" children are unable to withdraw from the parental conflicts and maintain their position of rejection of one parent throughout adolescence (Rand, 1997; Johnston, 1997).

In <u>Impasses of Divorce</u>, Johnston described children in "strong alignments" as forfeiting their childhood by "merging psychologically with a parent who was raging, paranoid, or sullenly depressed" (Johnston, 1988). Several factors contribute to the formation of these strong alignments in children. These factors are: 1) need to protect a parent who is either decompensating, depressed, panicky, or needy; 2) need to avoid the rage or rejection of the alienating parent; and 3) need to maintain the relationship the child is most afraid of losing (Johnston, 1988).

Extreme Alignments

Johnston and Roseby (1997) reserved Gardner's label "Parental Alienation Syndrome" for extreme alignment cases where children were refusing visitation. According to Johnston and Roseby (1997) these children in extreme alignments were viewed as "disturbed" by clinicians and teachers. These children "exhibit bizarre" and sometimes destructive behavior, including "unintegrated and chaotic attitudes with few workable defenses" (Johnston and Roseby, 1997). Sometimes alienating parents encourage and reinforce the child's use of pseudologia fantastica rather than providing reality to the child.

Johnston and Roseby opined, "rather than seeing this syndrome as being induced in the child by an alienating parent, as Gardner does, we propose that these 'unholy alliances' are a later manifestation of the failed separation-individuation process in especially vulnerable children, who have been exposed to disturbed family relationships during their early years" (Johnston and Roseby, 1997, p. 202).

Johnston and Roseby (1997) viewed these disturbed families as consisting of interparental conflict and a narcissistic disturbance in one or both parents. Additionally, Johnston and Roseby (1997) view parental alienation in early adolescents as failed separation-individuation from the alienating parent in the child's early years. This developmental failure adversely affects the adolescent's life and developing sense of self, resulting in failed separation-individuation.

Johnston and Roseby believe the most important factor in severe parental alienation cases is the child's vulnerability and receptivity to the alienating parent rather than "conscious, pernicious brainwashing" by an angry and bitter parent (Rand, 1997; Johnston & Roseby, 1997).

Rand states that "in contrast to Johnston and Roseby's view, mental health professionals practicing in the forensic arena often find evidence of substantial volitional activity on the part of the alienating parent in severe PAS" (Rand, 1997, p. 46). Whether these behaviors are "conscious" or "unconscious" the parent is responsible for these alienating behaviors which impact the child's relationship with the alienated parent.

Deviations From Developmental Norms

Children resistant to visitation deviate from usual developmental trends. Johnston and Roseby (1997) believe children who form consistent alignments with an alienating parent may not have separated psychologically from that parent. Contributing factors for children forming strong parent-child alignments before the "highest risk period of nine to twelve years of age" include: 1) failed separation-individuation process between parent and child; 2) intense parental pressure; and 3) a child who is more sensitive and vulnerable to parental conflict (Rand, 1997; Johnston and Roseby, 1997). However, some children become aligned with one parent with little overt conflict between the parents (Johnston, 1993). Even mild and subtle forms of parental influence can have significant effects (Clawar and Rivlin, 1991).

Child's Contributions in PAS

Gardner identifies a child as an active participant in the PAS. He identifies the most important contributing factor is that the child's basic psychological bond with the "loved parent" is stronger than with the "alienated parent" (Gardner, 1992). However, he maintains the child is psychologically bonded to both parents, but there is generally a stronger bond with the parent who was the primary caretaker in the child's earliest years. The campaign by the child then, is an attempt to maintain that parent-child bond to avoid disruption of that bond which may be threatened by custody litigation.

Children are naïve, simplistic and unsophisticated and cannot protect themselves with credible and meaningful "ammunition" against alienating parents. Alienating parents welcome the child's expression of resentments and complaints about the alienated parent. These inconsequential complaints by children and their absurdity are the "hallmark of the child's contribution" to the development of PAS (Gardner, 1992).

The child identifies with the alienating parent as PAS progresses and the alienated parent becomes viewed as loathsome and worthless. Deprived of the other parent for identification, the child may then switch to the alienating parent as the only parent to emulate. This may be a contributing factor to the child's exaggerated reactions to "any criticism the alienating parent may have about the alienated parent" (Gardner, 1992, p. 119). When the alienated parent criticizes the alienating parent, it is the same as criticizing the child in that child's mind. The child is identified with the "idealized" parent. In order to have their own needs met, the child must reflect whatever the "wounded parent needs and wants" (Johnston and Roseby, 1997). These children may become vigilant and highly attuned to the alienating parent. To disappoint or abandon the depressed, emotionally volatile, or raging parent could result in punishment, rejection, or being ignored (Johnston and Roseby, 1997). The child acts as though the alienating parent's survival depends on his or her caretaking. To betray that parent is "going over to the other side" (Johnson and Roseby, p. 198, 1997).

Divorce almost inevitably brings to children greater responsibilities. Children of chronically troubled parents carry this greater burden. These children may find themselves more alone and isolated. These children may be caring for a disorganized, depressed, dependent, enraged, or mentally or physically ill parent (Rand, 1997). Wallerstein and Blakeslee (1989) use the term "over-burdened child" to describe these problems. Wallerstein (1991) has encountered PAS, but prefers to conceptualize it from the "over-burdened" child framework rather than PAS.

The Alienated Parent in PAS

Children are twice as likely to form PAS type alignments with their mothers rather than with their fathers (Dunne, J., & Hederick, M., 1994; Wallerstein, J., & Kelly, J., 1980; Johnston, J., 1993). Similarly, fathers are more likely than mothers to become alienated parents.

The parent who has left the marriage is at higher risk for becoming an alienated parent (Rand, 1997). Johnston (1988) found high conflict families with unresolved anger and continued narcissistic injury of either parent to contribute significantly to the development of the child's rejection of one parent. Nicholas (1995) suggested the alienated parents may reinforce PAS by assuming an ambivalent or inconsistent stance after years of litigation. In other words, some alienated parents tend to become passive in their role of parenting, escalating the child's resistance to visitation with the alienated parent. Lund describes parents of moderate PAS families in which the alienated parent exhibited a distant, rigid style which was seen by the child as authoritarian when compared to the preferred parent, who was overly indulgent (Lund, M., 1995).

Alienated Parents Who are Falsely Accused

An allegation of child abuse, particularly molestation, quickly cuts off an alienated parent's access to the child, pending investigation (Rand, 1997). Sex abuse is often difficult, if not impossible to disprove and the accused parent may spend months and years trying without success to refute the charge with only supervised visitation with their child. Involvement of multiple agencies and lack of coordination between agencies and the courts lead to confusion and delays (Rand, 1997).

If the accused parent successfully refutes the accusing parent's allegations, that parent has lost valuable time with the child which may damage the parent-child relationship forever (Rand, 1997). Patterson stated, "we can never serve a child's best interests by denying him or her the love and affection of a parent who has been victimized by a lie" (Patterson, 1991, p. 941).

Characteristics of Alienated Parents

Alienated parents tend to display passive or dependent features whereas the alienating parent tends to display more histrionic behaviors (Blush, G., & Ross, K., 1987; 1990). Johnston and Roseby observed alienated parents as "rather inept and unempathic with their youngsters...the aligned parent is fueling the child's alienation...by counter-hostility and dogged pursuit of the child...(Johnston & Roseby, p.199, 1997). Johnston and Roseby observed alienated parents as not only hurt but outraged, by their child's challenge to their authority and lack of respect accorded them. Some alienated parents "pursue their children with a barrage of phone calls, letters, and unexpected appearances at activities, all of which feels very intrusive" (Johnston and

Roseby, p. 199, 1997). Unfortunately, the child's negative reactions are dismissed as "the other parent talking" (Johnson and Roseby, p. 199, 1997). Alienated parents need help in reaching out to their child in a nonintrusive, respectful manner with empathetic attunement.

Often, alienated parents are found to be emotionally and financially stable who functioned as a primary parent for their children prior to the separation, particularly in severe PAS (Sanders, C., 1993). Some alienated parents are fit and capable parents (Rand, 1997).

Characteristics of Alienating Parents

Alienating parents in custody cases were found to have significant emotional disturbance in contrast to some alienated parents who were deemed fit and capable of maintaining healthy parent-child bonds (Rand, 1997). In certain cases, the alienating parent who made false allegations of abuse was found to suffer from Delusional Disorder resulting in the alienated parents eventually receiving full custody in several cases (Rogers, M., 1992).

Gardner (1992) maintains the alienating parent's contributions and manifestations range from those that are entirely conscious to those that are deeply unconscious. These factors tend to shift over the passage of time and may become so automatic they are performed reflexively, without conscious appreciation of their detrimental effects. Gardner suggests it is usually the alienating parental input which is the predominant factor along with the programming which contributes to PAS. The alienating parent may maintain a campaign of denigration which may last for years. The alienated parent is vilified to the child with such terms as "adulterer," "abandoner" and "abuser" (Gardner, 1992; 1995).

Conclusion

PAS as formulated involves a cluster of child symptoms in divorce/custody. These symptoms are viewed as a syndrome because of the number of cases in which these symptoms share a common etiology (Rand, 1997). This is a combination of the alienating parent's influence and the child's "active" contributions to the campaign of denigration against the alienated parent (Rand, 1997).

However, researchers have readily refused to recognize the existence of PAS. Instead, other labels are attached to the demise of a once close parent-child relation. Some researchers have referred to the parental alienation "syndrome" as an "alignment." Neither this term or others adequately describe the behaviors Gardner observed.

Additionally, there has been little empirical evidence to support the efficacy of methods used by professionals in sorting out facts as they relate to PAS. Gardner is criticized because he self-published (Sullivan, M., 2000). Gardner called parental alienation a "syndrome" which led to more criticism and little acceptance of his work in the mental health community and the courts. However, PAS meets the definition of a syndrome. A syndrome is a "grouping of signs and symptoms that suggest a common underlying pathogenesis, course, familial pattern, or treatment selection" (DSM 4th.Ed, 1994).

The continuing reluctance of the research community and of the mental health community perpetuates growth of this syndrome and prolongs its life. This research will seek to provide solid additional answers about PAS as a "syndrome." Validation of parental alienation as a "syndrome" may hopefully lead to more refined understanding and treatment of this disorder.

PAS does not apply when children of a custody dispute become alienated from a parent because of that parent's lack of interest in the child or rejection of the child; significant deficits in an alienated parent's functioning; or the child is subjected to bonefide parental abuse or neglect (Rand, 1997). The benefit of using Dr. Gardner's terminology is that, where the facts of a given case support a diagnosis of PAS, there is a body of knowledge from which legal and/or therapeutic intervention are likely to be effective (Rand, 1997; Gardner, 1992).

However, Johnston (1993) suggests that it is not sufficient to lump mild and moderate PAS categories with "high conflict divorce in general." Johnston (1993) believes in its more severe forms, PAS is clearly distinctive, more destructive for children and families, and irreversible in its effects. Both Gardner and Johnston appear to agree severe PAS is identifiable and destructive irrespective of its name.

A child's developmental task is to integrate who they are in terms of mother and father and believe themselves to be a part of. Parental alienation is the "systematic destruction of a relationship with a parent (Sullivan, M., 2000). Dr. Sullivan strongly believes Dr. Gardner's definition of PAS cannot be "considered a syndrome because a syndrome[1] is 'medical,' Gardner is self-published and uses his testimony as an expert, and Gardner's conceptualization is inadequate (Sullivan, M. 2000[2])." Dr. Sullivan indicated a more useful conceptualization is to call this the "Alienated Child." Dr. Sullivan believes alienation begins with the child since there are other resistances to

[1] A syndrome is defined as a grouping of signs and symptoms, based upon their frequent occurrence that may suggest a common underlying pathogenesis, course, familial pattern, or treatment selection (DSM 4th Edition, 1994).

[2] Dr. Sullivan presented his preliminary study and presentation at a workshop for attorneys and evaluators sponsored by the Sacramento Valley Psychological Association, 2000.

visitation or contact with one parent. Dr. Sullivan indicated an 18-month old would not fit Gardner's criteria. This is correct, but this is only common sense and; Dr. Gardner does not purport to suggest this possibility. An 18-month old is not cognitively able to participate in any form of alienation and to suggest this is absurd. Dr. Sullivan suggests we begin to "look at the resistances of why children refuse visitation since it may not be alienation." However, Dr. Sullivan does appear to agree with Dr. Gardner's severe alienation category.

Dr. Gardner acknowledges there are good reasons a child resists visitation. Less than adequate caregiving or abuse by a parent can result in strong resistance by the child and there is no implication there is PAS existing. A good evaluator can deduce parental capacities and the reasons for the child's resistance, including resistance which is due to PAS. Gardner does not purport resistance due to abuse, mild to severe, is ever the cause of PAS. To infer otherwise is to have misunderstood Gardner's concepts. It is quite simple to sort out resistances to visitation when there has been genuine abuse; it is not simple to sort out children who resist because of genuine PAS. Dr. Gardner deserves credit for recognition and defining PAS.

Each parent attempts to induce the child's loyalty towards him or her in the majority of custody disputes. When these indoctrinations become strong, PAS symptoms may develop in the child. Gardner believes the stronger the programming; the greater the likelihood the child will create contributions of his or her own (Gardner, 1995). A diagnosis of PAS is then justified. Gardner (1995) believes it is important to understand that the determinant as to whether a Parental Alienation Syndrome is categorized as mild, moderate or severe is its manifestations in the *child*. Parents designated as moderate or even severe programmers may not be successful in producing significant symptoms of alienation in the child. This may be due to the child's attachment and bonding with the alienated parent. Additionally, there are factors in children which lead to PAS. These factors are: 1) child's gullibility; 2) child's intelligence (the brighter the child the less likely he or she will believe the absurd criticisms); 3) personality of the child; 4) independent thinking by the child; 5) self sufficiency of the child; and 6) the age of the child (Rand, 1997).

Overall, Gardner's observations in 1985 paved the way for defining behaviors and symptoms in both children and parents never before accounted for in high conflict custody cases. Parent-child relations can now be salvaged if properly identified and intervention begun. Continued research in this area is essential. The mental health community has been limited by the lack of published data to support observations of PAS.

CHAPTER THREE

METHODOLOGY

<u>Overview</u>

In the first chapter of this dissertation, general definitions of the following concepts were given: Parental Alienation Syndrome (PAS), Mild, Moderate and Severe. Additionally, manifestations of and definitions of the characteristics and symptomology observed in children and parents with PAS were described.

In this Chapter, operational definitions of these concepts are presented along with a description of the methods used to measure them. The following topics were covered including selection of the court-referred cases and the data obtained from these cases; procedures used to collect the information sought from each case; the methods used to review the data; description of instrumentation used to collect data; the method used for developing the criteria used for collecting this data; discussion of data processing, including recordation of data; and the inherent limitations in this study.

<u>Restatement of the Problem</u>

The norm for children of divorce is to continue to love and long for *both* parents despite the passage of time subsequent to separation or divorce (Rand, 1997). In 1985, the concept of Parental Alienation Syndrome (PAS) was introduced. PAS refers to the child's denigrating and rejecting a previously loved parent in the context of divorce or custody (Rand, 1997). During child custody evaluations, Dr. Gardner observed that children were preoccupied with denigrating one parent, even to the point of expressing hatred toward a once loved parent (Gardner, 1992; Rand, 1997).

Legal, psychological, and psychiatric communities still "cringe" when PAS is suggested outright or is part of a court report. The psychology community denounces PAS because it is not a valid syndrome. Some researchers believe a syndrome belongs in the medical community (Sullivan, M., 2000). This study will seek to determine whether there may be support for PAS within the legal context of custody/divorce, as first presented in 1985.

Statement of Research Questions

Thirty court-referred cases involving 59 children were reviewed to determine the "presence" or "absence" of PAS. The present study reviewed the case data to determine if the existence of PAS in custody cases can be verified.

The research questions are: Can observations of Parental Alienation Syndrome be supported? Descriptive statistics were used to answer this question as to the presence or absence of PAS symptomology. Secondarily, is there a difference between the three groups of children in this study? ANOVA one-way analysis of variance was used here. Next, the difference in the demographics including race, gender, and age was examined. Nonparametric statistics were used here. If the data of the children supports Gardner's findings, then Gardner's observations and findings are valid.

Operational Definition of Variables

This section will operationally define the variables used in this study. They include "PAS: mild, moderate and severe (parental symptoms and child's symptoms)," "paranoia," "anger," "programming the child," "desire for vengeance," "sexual abuse/physical abuse allegations," and "noncompliance with court orders," "intractable" custody disputes, "routine" court proceedings, and "conflict."

Operational definitions for the varying degrees of PAS are set forth below, with the cases categorized as "mild," "moderate" or "severe" based on the presence or absence of certain "guidepost" behavioral patterns or thought processes. The behavioral patterns or thought processes (i.e. a desire for vengeance, programming of the children and the presence or absence of anger) are manifested in an infinite variety of ways. These manifestations are observed in the clinical setting, pursuant to which certain conclusions are drawn as to whether the "guidepost" behavioral patterns or thought processes are in fact present.

1. Mild PAS, Parent's Symptoms

Operationally, mild PAS in parents is as follows: 1) The alienating parent may have a desire for vengeance, i.e., alleges the other parent does not take 'you' to school on time with the intent to modify custody; 2) participates in slight programming of the child, i.e., your "dad never really cared about 'us;'" 3) is angry, i.e., continues to verbalize past wrongs by the other parent; 4) has a strong preference for sole custody or primary physical custody, i.e., will not negotiate a shared parenting agreement to include the other parent, but does believe the alienated parent should be involved in the child's life.

An alienating parent with mild PAS understands complete alienation from the other parent is not in the best interests of the child. The parent negotiates for visitation with the other parent rather than "no" contact. No paranoia exists here, but there is a desire for primary physical custody with limited visitation. For example, the father has every other weekend, with primary custody to the mother. There is a desire to keep the other parent in the child's life, but only marginally. For example, a mother after eight years of separation from the father, attempted to return to court to reduce the father's parenting time because she did not believe father really "cared about the minors" the way "normal" fathers care. The mother wanted the father to remain in the minors' lives

because she believed the father should be a part of the minors' life, but a minimal part.

The programming of the children presented itself because the children, too, did not

believe the father "cared enough." The mother and minors were primarily bonded and

there was a strong desire to maintain this bond on both the part of the mother and the

minors. The mother in this case was very angry with the father for leaving. The mother

complied with all court orders, but there were frequent attempts to interfere with the

father's visitation and convince the minors' the father did not really "care about them."

2. Moderate PAS, Parents' Symptoms

The parents of children in this category are more disturbed than the parents in

the mild category. In these cases, "rage from rejection" by the other parent is more

important than the paranoid projection contribution (Gardner, 1992). The parents in this

category denigrate the other parent, are angry, and desire to withhold the children from

the alienated parent as a vengeance maneuver. These parents frequently do not comply

with court orders, but will comply with threats of sanctions or a modification in the

custody schedule, including a reversal of custody.

These parents denigrate the other parent by making repeated negative comments

about the other parent, usually stated with disdain and anger. For example, a parent

may repeatedly state to the child some "fact" about the other parent which will hurt the

child, i.e. "your father never really liked going to your soccer games anyway."

Additionally, these parents will find a variety of excuses to interfere with or

circumvent visitation with the alienated parent. Commonly, these parents will obtain a

medical "excuse" as to why they are "unable" to comply with court ordered exchanges.

These parents' reality is sufficiently intact such that they are able to differentiate between sex/abuse allegations which are preposterous and those which may have some validity. A parent will not make allegations of molestation against the other parent upon discovering a fact such as "daddy takes a bath with me," but would if told "daddy touched my privates."

For example, a moderate PAS case may be referred where the alienating parent is desiring to protect the minor until the investigation regarding a sex abuse allegation is complete. Now, however, the alienating parent could begin to program the child to fear the alienated parent because of this "ordeal." The alienating parent does not believe the sex abuse occurred, but rather uses it as a tool to program the child to fear the alienated parent and draw the child closer. The alienating parent may overtly or covertly suggest to the child that there is some reason to fear the other parent.

3. Severe PAS, Parents' Symptoms

The parents of these children are often fanatics. They attempt to prevent visitation with the alienated parent and are obsessed with rage toward the alienated parent. In many cases, these parents are paranoid. For example, during interviews, the parent rages incessantly about the past and current perceived or actual inadequacies of the other parent. The same actual or perceived inadequacies are unrelentingly voiced over and over, beyond any rational or reasonable point. These parents do not respond to logic and will not comply with court orders, including threats of contempt.

For example, the parental symptoms, in the severe PAS category are denigrating and vilifying the alienated parent in front of the children. The denigration and programming by the alienating parent does not cease despite court warnings and interventions.

In one case involving two female children ages six years and eight years, sex-abuse allegations were made against the alienated parent. None of the allegations were substantiated. The allegations continued with more investigation, but still no substantiation. The alienated parent's visitation was expanded. Within six months, the alienating parent made several more sex-abuse allegations and continually involved the children in her scenarios. The children began to "parrot" the alienating parent, stating "he just wants money," "he scares us," and "he touched us with the bar of soap." Custody was reversed in favor of the alienated parent.

4. Mild PAS, Child's Symptoms

The child maintains affection for both parents. The child has contact and visitation with both parents. The child may have a stronger psychological bond with the alienating parent. This may allow a mildly alienating parent some ability to induce the child to want more time with that parent, but not to the degree that it significantly harms the child's relationship with the other parent. Children might state, "Daddy is nice, but I want more time with mommy and daddy doesn't need me as much."

5. Moderate PAS, Child's Symptoms

Children in this category denigrate the alienated parent by making negative comments about that parent. The child's denigration of his/her parent are frequently identical to those made by the alienating parent. However, these children can still frequently show affection when alone with the alienated parent. These children are more likely to give up their scenarios when alone with the alienated parent, especially for long periods (Gardner, 1992).

For example, after five years of a highly contested custody dispute, three children were interviewed separately. The children in varying degrees vilified their

father, expressed extreme fear of, and little desire to be alone with the alienated parent.
The alienating parent did not comply with the court order despite threats of contempt.
Custody was reversed and the minors gave up their derogatory and vilifying scenarios
of the alienated parent almost immediately. Their relationship was fairly normal within
three weeks and within six months healthy.

6. Severe PAS, Child's Symptoms

This category is defined as children who strongly resist visitation with the
alienated parent, show no guilt or remorse about their behavior, vilify the alienated
parent, and have strong feelings of anger toward the alienated parent. The children are
often so angry at the alienated parent that they refuse to call that parent "mom" or "dad,"
instead insisting on calling the parent by their first name (i.e. Carol or John). For
example, two female children presented with symptoms of severe PAS. These two
children were seen individually and each child called their father by his first name,
explained his inadequacies and incompetence, and refused visitation despite court
orders to the contrary. "John (Father) can't do anything right; we don't trust him."

7. Paranoia

Parents exhibiting paranoia do not respond to logic, confrontations with reality,
or reason. They truly believe the most preposterous scenarios. For example, police and
Child Protective Services social workers may find no evidence of any sexual or physical
abuse despite allegations to the contrary. The alienating parent is not able to alter their
beliefs or reduce their commitment to the campaign of denigration, false allegations, and
rage.

For example, in one case, a mother was certain that her daughters had been
molested by the father at ages two and three and one-half years. This scenario

continued for five years with multiple investigations by the Police Department and Child Protective Services, all molestation unsubstantiated. The children repeated the same scenario about the molestation that the mother did. Reversal of custody with supervised visitation to the mother resulted in escalating mother's belief system. Another allegation against the father for molestation was made three months later despite the reversal of custody.

8. Programming the Child

A parent denigrates and criticizes the alienated parent overtly and covertly. The programming is conscious and/or unconscious on the part of the alienating parent. For example, the parent comments "you always have a stomach ache when you return from your mother's; she just does not know how to take care of you." This would not have happened if she had not left "us." Messages such as these are repeated over and over in a variety of ways and situations. The child can become well programmed if so inclined.

9. Allegations of Sexual or other Abuse

False allegations of sexual abuse occur in the more severe PAS cases. The alienating parent creates a scenario when the alleged abuse took place and repeats the scenario over and over to the child often expanding the facts. Again, the four-year-old boy who stated over and over his father put his "fingers in his bottom and rolled him in a sheet" truly believed this occurred because of the repetition of the scenario by his mother. The mother's extended family began to repeat the scenario. All allegations were unfounded. Usually, the alienating parent's belief system that the molestation or abuse occurred is not altered and their discussion about the abuse to the child is not diminished without legal and/or mental health intervention.

10. "Intractable" Custody Disputes

Intractable custody disputes involve a custody case in which the parents cannot resolve their conflict despite at least two prior court referrals for mediation and/or evaluation.

11. "Routine" Court Proceedings

Routine court proceedings are typical in parents who desire the best interests of their children. These parents agree to share parenting with or without legal intervention or reach agreement with assistance from the court, attorneys, or a mediator. These parties do not end up with repeated court hearings, mediations, or evaluations.

12. "Conflict "

Conflict is operationally defined as a custody dispute between parents which has not been resolved by routine court proceedings. Multiple court proceedings indicate intractable conflict. For example, the parents of triplets have been through three custody evaluations within 18 months with three different evaluators. One parent in the case refused to follow court orders regarding the visitation schedule. Conflicted custody is generally two or more referrals to the court within a 12-month period.

Discussion of Data Processing

The thirty court cases (each parent and each child) in this study were categorized based on the PAS parental and the PAS child behaviors. Each parent and each child was placed in the appropriate category: mild, moderate or severe based on their behaviors and the criteria met. Each parent and each child had data collected, including gender, age, race, behaviors, and symptoms prior to the study. Each child and each parent was then placed in the appropriate category depending on their symptoms/behaviors.

Descriptive statistics described potential differences in the number of symptoms observed in the children and parents. Demographics from each group were compared. This data was examined using nonparametric one-way analysis statistics. The data was compiled and then compared and described whether or not these thirty court referred cases support the existence of PAS.

Selection of Data

Thirty court-referred cases for therapy, evaluation, or mediation were selected for this study. The cases were referred by the court because of continuing conflict between the parents. The cases have been in the court system previously (two or more times) and were referred to this researcher because of intractable conflict between the parents. All cases are highly contested custody disputes. The cases reviewed were referred within the last 24 months commencing January 1, 1998. The thirty cases were assigned to either the mild, moderate, or severe category based on the PAS criteria of the parents. The children's data for each group was reviewed using the PAS criteria for mild, moderate or severe to determine the children's' responses. Demographic data was compared in each group.

Description of Research Design

The cases used in this study were cases with at least two prior court referrals, and were referred to the investigator by the court because of intractable conflict and custody dispute. The cases were placed into one of three categories (mild, moderate or severe) based on criteria from the description for parental symptomology for PAS. The cases will date back to January 1998.

Once the cases were categorized based upon the parental PAS criteria, each child from each case was then categorized into the children's criteria for mild, moderate, or severe PAS. Each case was examined to determine the level of PAS associated behaviors exhibited by the parents and children. Then the three groups of children were compared to confirm the existence and severity of PAS within and between the three groups.

Statement of Hypotheses

The null hypothesis is that there is no significant relationship between the mild, moderate, or severe PAS category of the children to support the existence of PAS. Alternatively, there is a primary hypothesis that there is a relationship between the findings of this study and the criteria for PAS. It is expected that a mild PAS parent will produce a mild PAS child and that a moderate and severe PAS parent will produce a moderate and severe PAS child respectively.

ANOVA was used for assessing the statistical significance of the relationship between the independent variable and dependent variables (Vogt, W., 1999). ANOVA one-way was used because it applies to a design with one independent variable (Levin, I., Hinrich, J., 1995). The independent variable in this study is the existence or not of PAS in the children in the case studies reviewed, and the dependent variable is the total score using the criteria of PAS and the answers to the individual questions. One-way analysis of variance applies to this research design because there is one independent variable: the existence or not of PAS in the children. The ANOVA procedure was selected to examine potential differences in the number of symptoms observed in children in the mild, moderate, and severe groups.

Each child's history was reviewed to determine what happens to the children in this study. Children whose parents have mild PAS were compared to children whose parents have moderate and severe PAS. The severity of the symptoms of the children in each category were examined to determine if this research data supports the presence or absence of PAS.

The secondary hypothesis examines whether there is a difference between children's symptoms and their parent's if they are in the severe PAS category compared to those children whose parents are in the mild and moderate PAS categories. One-way analysis of variance were used to compare these groups.

Each parent and each child had demographic data collected, including age, gender, and race. This demographic data were examined and compared among the groups. The third hypothesis is that there is no significant difference between the demographic characteristics of children and their PAS category. Each parent and each child had demographic data collected including age, gender, and race. Nonparametric statistics were used to examine the demographic data.

Each child's case was reviewed to determine the number of symptoms exhibited in each child. The PAS criteria for the children were used to determine the level of severity of the children's' responses. The children's symptoms for each category were reviewed and compared. Each group was reviewed using nonparametric, one-way analysis variance statistics. Descriptive statistics, described above, were used to describe this study's findings for the "presence" or "absence" of PAS. Measures of variability in the categories were described. The data obtained from the thirty-case sample describes parents using the parental criteria for PAS: mild, moderate and severe. Data from the criteria for children's symptoms with PAS: mild, moderate, and severe was reviewed for each case. Nonparametric statistics were used to analyze the difference between the children's groups as well as the demographic data obtained.

The procedures used for organizing, collecting, and graphing data from the thirty cases is fully described. If the data for the parents is sound and the data from the children supports Gardner's findings, then Gardner's observations and findings are sound.

Description of Children's' PAS Symptoms

The symptoms for <u>Mild</u> PAS in the child is based on the following symptomology: child maintains visitation with the alienated parent, there is expression of affection towards the alienated parent, especially when alone with that parent, and expresses positive feelings about the alienated parent. The verbal child parrots mildly negative statements about the alienated parent but continues visitation. For example, the child states "dad is boring or my dad never takes us anywhere." However, the child is engaged and happy during conjoint interviews with the alienated parent. There is not a ruptured parent-child relationship; it remains intact.

The criteria for <u>Moderate</u> PAS in the child is based on the following: vilification of the alienated parent, anger towards the alienated parent, expression of affection toward the alienated parent <u>only</u> when alone with that parent, and resisted visitation with the alienated parent. The child resists visitation by making excuses not to go to the alienated parent's home. The child vilifies by name-calling, i.e., "he's stupid, he's always abused us, or she's always hitting." The child is adamant about their negative characterizations. Their statements are similar to the alienating parent's statements about the alienated parent.

<u>Severe</u> PAS in the child is categorized as follows: the child strongly resists visitation with the alienated parent, the child vilifies and denigrates the alienated parent, the child expresses anger and no positive feelings towards the alienated parent;

however, there may be vague ambivalence if alone with the alienated parent. The child

frequently refuses all visitation. Visitation may be enforced if supervised and under

court order. The child states, "I hate her/him." There is a rupture of the parent-child

relationship; contact is frequently stopped between the alienated parent and the child.

Description of Instrumentation

The instrumentation used in this study is listed in the Appendixes C and D. The

chart for collecting data from the children and parents using the PAS criteria was

designed by this investigator. Additionally, there are "interview/evaluation" forms

used during parent and child interviews included for review. See Appendix A, Initial

Intake, Parental Interview and Appendix B, Interview with Minor Child.

Importance of this Research

There has been little empirical evidence to support the efficacy of methods

typically used by professionals in sorting out facts as they relate to PAS. Diagnosis of

and acceptance of PAS is very important in the field of custody and divorce. Detection

of PAS and an understanding of appropriate remedial interventions to restore the child's

relationship with an alienated parent is in the best interests of children. This research

may lend support for PAS. The professionals who now shy away from diagnosing PAS

may find greater support for their findings of PAS in the legal and mental health

communities.

Methodological Assumptions and Limitations

There are limitations to this study. More specifically, to assume a small sample

(n=30) can be generalized, necessitates assumption that the sample is representative of

PAS in intractable custody disputes. The cases reviewed are court referred only.

Examination of intractable, custody dispute cases only creates a restriction of the range of the cases analyzed. Therefore, generalization may be limited.

Ethical Assurances

Confidentiality was maintained at all times. This researcher did not have contact with subjects, only the data contained in their files. The information letter (Appendix E) has been sent to all persons informing them of this study and that data from their records were included.

CHAPTER FOUR

ANALYSIS AND RESULTS

<u>Overview</u>

This study examined Parental Alienation Syndrome (PAS), and sought to determine whether there is support for the existence of this syndrome. The cases used in this study had at least two prior court referrals because of intractable conflict.

The parents in each case were categorized using the PAS symptomology and were placed into the mild, moderate, or severe category. Once the parents were categorized, each child from each case family was categorized using the children's criteria of symptoms for mild, moderate, or severe PAS.

The behaviors and feelings of these children were then examined for: anger, expression of affection, denigration, positive feelings, and visitation with the alienated parent. The three groups of children (mild, moderate, and severe) were then compared to see if there were any differences in the number of symptoms exhibited by these children. In other words, did the children in the severe group have more symptoms or negative behaviors than the children in the mild group?

The category of the parent(s) was then related to the category of the child(ren) to see if there was any relationship. Behaviors and feelings of the mild PAS parents are: paranoia, programming the child, anger, false allegations of sexual/physical abuse, a strong preference for primary physical custody, desire for vengeance, and belief the alienated parent should be involved in the child's life. The categories of behaviors for moderate PAS parents are: paranoia, programming the child, anger, false allegations of sexual/physical abuse, unreceptive to complying with court orders, desire for vengeance, and interferes with visitation. The categories of behaviors for severe PAS

57

parents consist of: paranoia, programming the child, anger, false allegations of sexual/physical abuse, fanatic to prevent/interrupt visitation, desire for vengeance, and unreceptive to complying with court orders.

The three groups of children (mild, moderate, and severe) were then compared to see if there were any differences in the number of symptoms exhibited by these children. In other words, did the children in the severe group have more symptoms or negative behaviors than the children in the moderate group or than the children in the mild group.

Findings

This study also looked at the degree of alienation on the part of the alienating parent and relates it to the degree of negative behaviors expressed by his or her child. Dr. Gardner believes that the amount of alienation experienced by a child is directly related to the amount of hostility expressed by the custodial parent towards the noncustodial parent.

Since the purpose of this study was to determine whether there is support for the Parental Alienation Syndrome, a second element of the study looked at the relationship between the findings of this study and the PAS criteria based on the children's symptoms. One might anticipate that a mildly alienated child should come from a mildly alienating parent with mild symptoms. This relationship would be expected to apply to moderate and severe PAS.

The data from this study, indicates that parents in the mild PAS category have children who exhibit fewer negative behaviors towards the alienated parent. For example, there were 22 children in the mild "anger" group with no anger expressed toward the alienated parent. Contrarily, in the severe "anger" group, 18 children out of

20 children expressed anger towards the alienated parent and more of their parents were angry. This is significant. In the moderate group, 10 children expressed anger and 7 children did not express anger toward the alienated parent.

Additionally, one child out of 22 children in the mild group refused visitation whereas 17 out of 20 children in the severe group refused visitation with the alienated parent. The parents in this category also had more negative behaviors. This indicates the more negative the parent's behaviors, the more disruption to the alienated parent's relationship with the child. This data supports the research questions discussed in Chapter 1: 1) this study does appear to support PAS using the specific children's' and parents' criteria to identify the existence and degree of PAS; and 2) the data supports the differences between the three groups of children using the PAS criteria of mild, moderate and severe symptoms in both the children and parents.

The milder group of children had fewer negative behaviors and a relationship with the alienated parent. However, the severe group of children had more negative behaviors and greater resistance to a parent-child relation with the alienated parent. The more negative symptoms the parents had, the more negative the behaviors of the child.

Overall, children in the severe group had more negative behaviors. Therefore, the parents in the mild category had children with mild symptoms. Their parent-child relations with the alienated parent were more positive with fewer negative behaviors. The children whose parents were in the severe category had more negative behaviors. Additionally, the children of these parents were identified as having more parent-child problems and resistance to visitation with the alienated parent.

The study also looked at the relationship between the findings of this study and the criteria for PAS based on the children's symptoms. The data indicates there is a relationship between the alienating parent's behaviors and their child's negative behaviors towards the alienated parent. One might anticipate that a mildly alienated child should come from a mildly alienating parent with mild symptoms, a moderately alienated child should come from a moderately alienating parent, and a severely alienated child should come from a severely alienating parent.

The differences in the number of negative behaviors towards the alienated parent were compared between the three groups of children. The children's symptoms and behaviors, based upon the PAS children's criteria for mild, moderate or severe symptoms and behaviors, determined the child's group. ANOVA one-way analysis of variance was used to compare these three groups.

ANOVA was used to compare the absence or presence of PAS symptoms. More specifically, this was used to assess the variance between and within the three groups of the children to determine the number of symptoms in each child, in each group, and the presence or absence of PAS. The data found the more negative behaviors the child expressed, the more likely severe PAS was present. Contrarily, children with fewer negative behaviors were in the mild group. There is a relationship between the negative behaviors in the parents and the negative behaviors in the child.

The data indicates there were more children in the mild category which had visitation with the alienated parent than expected and there were fewer children in the severe group than expected who did not have visitation with the alienated parent. The data supports a significant difference between the mild group and severe group of children.

The difference in the demographics, including race, gender, and age was compared between the groups of children. The third hypothesis is that there is no significant difference between the demographic characteristics of children and their PAS

category. Descriptive statistics were used to compare the demographics, including race,

gender, and age. There were 30 families and 59 children. No child under age 5 years

was in the severe group.

Demographics

Age

There are a total of 59 children in this study. In the mild PAS children's group,

there were 22 children; in the moderate PAS children's group, there were 17 children;

and in the severe PAS group, there were 20 children. The children's ages range from 2 to

17 years with an average age of 9.6 years, (SD = 3.5). With regard to the three groups,

the average age of the children in the mild group is 10.7 years, 9.3 years in the moderate

group and 8.9 years in the severe group.

It is significant that very young children, under age 5 years, were not found in

the severe group. Children under age 5 years may lack the psychological and emotional

maturity to be programmed.

Gender

There were 26 male children and 33 female children in this study. There were 12

males in the mild group, 6 males in the moderate group and 8 males in the severe group.

Regarding females, there were 10 in the mild group, 11 in the moderate group and 12 in

the severe group. More females were alienated than males. More mothers have been

found to alienate children. Female children may have a stronger psychological bond

with the alienating parent (mother) or identify with a same-sex parent, particularly

during latency and pre-adolescence.

Race

There were 49 Caucasians, 6 African-Americans and 4 Asian children. In the mild children's group, there are 14 Caucasians, 6 African-Americans, and 2 Asian children. In the moderate group, there are 15 Caucasians, and 2 Asian children. In the severe group, there are 20 Caucasian children. In sum, there were 83.1% Caucasian; 10.2% African-American and 8.2% Asian. There are no statistically significant differences in this category. There were too many variables not controlled to significantly determine whether one culture is prone to PAS over another culture.

Visitation with the Alienated Parent

In Table 1, Chi-square = 28.39 (df = 2), p < .05. This is significant because the

three groups were statistically different with regard to visitation. Therefore, the null

hypothesis of no difference between the three groups is rejected. As the degree of

severity increased (refusal to visit), the percent of children visiting the alienated parent

decreased. More children (21 with an expected count of 13.1) in the mild group had

visitation with the alienated parent than in the severe group (3 with an expected count

of 11.9). In the moderate group, (11 children with an expected count of 10.1) had

visitation with the alienated parent.

TABLE 1

Mild PAS vs. Moderate PAS vs. Severe PAS Visitation with AP[1]

| | | | VISITATION WITH AP[1] | | |
			0=NO	1=YES	Total
Mild PAS vs. Moderate PAS vs. Severe PAS	1 Mild PAS	Count	1	21	22
		Expected Count	8.9	13.1	22.0
	2 Moderate PAS	Count	6	11	17
		Expected Count	6.9	10.1	17.0
	3 Severe PAS	Count	17	3	20
		Expected Count	8.1	11.9	20.0
Total		Count	24	35	59
		Expected Count	24.0	35.0	59.0

[1] AP = Alienated Parent

Express Affection with the Alienated Parent

In Table 2, Chi-square = 6.49 (df = 2), p < .05. The three groups were statistically

different with regard to expression of affection. The null hypothesis of no difference

between the three groups is rejected. As the degree of severity increased, the percent of

children expressing affection to the alienated parent decreased. More children (18 with

an expected count of 14.2) in the mild group had expressed affection to the alienated

parent than in the severe group (9 with an expected count of 12.9). In the moderate

group, (11 children with an expected count of 10.1) had visitation with the alienated

parent. There are no statistical differences in the moderate group.

TABLE 2

Mild PAS vs. Moderate PAS vs. Severe PAS Express Affection with AP[1]

			Express Affection with AP[1]		
			0=NO	1=YES	Total
Mild PAS vs. Moderate PAS vs. Severe PAS	1 Mild PAS	Count	4	18	22
		Expected Count	7.8	14.2	22.0
	2 Moderate PAS	Count	6	11	17
		Expected Count	6.1	10.9	17.0
	3 Severe PAS	Count	11	9	20
		Expected Count	7.1	12.9	20.0
Total		Count	21	38	59
		Expected Count	21.0	38.0	59.0

<u>Anger at Alienated Parent</u>

In Table 3, Chi-square = 35.27, (df = 2) p < .05. The three groups were

statistically different with respect to the level of anger expressed towards the alienated

parent. No children in the mild group expressed anger. However, in the severe group

18 out of 20 children expressed anger at the alienated parent. It is significant that <u>no</u>

<u>children</u> in the mild group expressed anger at the alienated parent. Examination of the

results reveals no children in the mild group expressed anger whereas more children in

the severe group expressed anger. Therefore the difference in the three groups is

between the mild and severe groups. The null hypothesis of no difference between the

three groups is rejected. In the moderate group, 7 children out of 17 were angry at the

alienated parent.

TABLE 3

Mild PAS vs. Moderate PAS vs. Severe PAS <u>Anger at AP[1]</u>

			Anger at AP[1]		
			0=NO	1=YES	TOTAL
Mild PAS vs. Moderate PAS vs. Severe PAS	1 Mild PAS	Count	22	0	22
		Expected Count	11.6	10.4	22.0
	2 Moderate PAS	Count	7	10	17
		Expected Count	8.9	8.1	17.0
	3 Severe PAS	Count	2	18	20
		Expected Count	10.5	9.5	20.0
TOTAL		Count	31	28	59
		Expected Count	31.0	28.0	59.0

TABLE 3 continued

Chi-square Tests

	Value	Df	Asymp. Sig. (2-sided)
Pearson Chi-square	35.268[a]	2	.000
Likelihood Ratio	45.601	2	.000
Linear-by-Linear Association	33.759	1	.000
n of Valid Cases	59		

a. 0 cells (.0%) have expected count less than 5. The minimum expected count is 8.07.

Denigration of Alienated Parent

In Table 4, Chi-square = 20.86, (df = 2) p < .05. There were fewer children in the mild group who exhibited behaviors of denigration towards the alienated parent. However, in the severe group, more children than the expected count exhibited symptoms of denigration toward the alienated parent. This is statistically significant. The null hypothesis is rejected. In this case, the three groups were statistically different with regard to denigration. As the degree of severity increased, the number of children denigrating the alienated parent increased. The moderate group had 10 children who exhibited behaviors of denigration as opposed to 6.3 expected.

TABLE 4

Mild PAS vs. Moderate PAS vs. Severe PAS Denigration of AP[1]

| | | | Denigration of AP[1] | | Total |
			0=NO	1=YES	
Mild PAS vs. Moderate PAS vs. Severe PAS	1 Mild PAS	Count	22	0	22
		Expected Count	13.8	8.2	22.0
	2 Moderate PAS	Count	7	10	17
		Expected Count	10.7	6.3	17.0
	3 Severe PAS	Count	8	12	20
		Expected Count	12.5	7.5	20.0
Total		Count	37	22	59
		Expected Count	37.0	22.0	59.0

Chi-square Test

	Value	df	Asymp. Sig. (2-sided)
Pearson Chi-square	20.86[a]	2	.000
Likelihood Ratio	27.98	2	.000
Linear-by Linear Assn.	16.28	1	.000
N of Valid Cases	59		

a. 0 cells (.0%) have expected count less than 5. The minimum expected count is 6.34.

The Sum of Children's Behaviors

Table 5 is the last analysis of the number of behaviors expressing PAS
(refusal of visitation, affection, anger, positive feelings and denigration) which were
summed to obtain a total number of symptoms observed for each child. The groups
were then compared to determine if there were any differences with regard to the total
number of behaviors. To accomplish this, anger and denigration were recoded.
Therefore, a 1 = positive or presence of behaviors and a 0 = negative or absence of
behaviors so the sum of all behaviors is a higher value. A negative number is
representative of fewer behaviors. One-way analysis of variance was used for this
comparison.

In Table 5, the children in the mild PAS group expressed fewer negative
behaviors than the moderate or severe PAS groups. The mild PAS children expressed
more positive behaviors toward the alienated parent or less negative behaviors toward
the alienated parent, $F = 2.977$ (2, 56), $p < .05$. The more severe the behaviors toward the
alienated parent, the fewer positive behaviors on the part of the children. The null
hypothesis of no difference between the three groups is rejected. In this study, the three
groups were statistically different for each category (anger, refusal to visit, denigration,
affection, and positive feelings). As the degree of severity increased, the more negative
the child's behavior, and the percent of the children visiting the alienating parent
decreased.

TABLE 5

Sum of <u>Visitation, Affection, Positive Feelings, Anger, Denigration</u>

	N	Mean	Std. Deviation
1 Mild PAS	22	4.5455	0.7385
2 Moderate PAS	17	2.8235	1.9441
3 Severe PAS	20	1.3000	1.3018
Total	59	2.9492	1.9246

Analysis and Evaluation of Findings

There has been little empirical evidence to support the efficacy of methods

typically used by professionals in sorting out facts as they relate to PAS and their cases.

Dr. Gardner recognized the symptoms of PAS and categorized them into three groups.

This study's research findings appear to support PAS's existence. There is a

statistical relationship between the "anger" of the parent and its effect upon the

child(ren). As the parent became more hostile toward the other parent, the child(ren)

became/exhibited greater alienation toward the alienated parent.

The three groups of children were statistically different regarding the behaviors

reviewed. Children in the mild group typically had fewer negative behaviors and more

visitation with the alienated parent. Conversely, children in the severe group had more

negative behaviors and less visitation with the alienated parent. There is a clear

distinction between the mild and severe groups of children. PAS is such a serious

disruption of the parent-child relationship that earlier intervention can now be

recognized and accepted.

Demographics were not significant as a predictor of the severity of PAS in this

study. However, it is significant to note the minimum age in the severe category is 5

years, and in the mild and moderate categories, the minimum age drops to age 2 years old. There were more females in the moderate and severe categories than males. There were 83.1% Caucasian, 0.2% African-American, and 8.2% Asian children.

CHAPTER FIVE

CONCLUSIONS, LIMITATIONS, AND RECOMMENDATIONS

Summary

The Parental Alienation Syndrome (PAS) has been misinterpreted, misunderstood, and at times highly criticized. Legal, psychological, and psychiatric communities still "cringe" when PAS is suggested outright or as part of a court report. Parental Alienation Syndrome is probably pervasive in high conflict custody disputes. The most significant finding in this study is the difference between the severe PAS category and the mild PAS category. The more negative behaviors the child exhibited, the more negative the parental behaviors and the more severe the PAS.

It is the norm for children of divorce to continue to love and long for both parents despite the passage of time. PAS is used to refer to a child's denigrating and rejecting a previously loved parent in the context of divorce or custody dispute (Gardner, 1992).

Additionally, a mild case of PAS may need additional investigation because the resistance of a child to visit a parent may be due in part to developmental tasks or other parent-child relations. Mental health professionals recognize this. Additionally, a mild PAS parent may have a very strong psychological bond with the child, and there may be resistance to separation. That parent simply may not recognize the importance of the child's relationship with the other parent. Actual child maltreatment or abuse must first be ruled out before proceeding with the PAS diagnosis.

There has been little empirical evidence to support the efficacy of methods typically used by professionals to sort out facts as they relate to PAS. This study found

72

more negative symptoms and behaviors (towards the alienated parent) in the severe and moderate PAS group than in the mild group of children. Both the moderate and severe groups of children had more anger, more resistance to visitation , and less affection towards the alienated parent. This study found that the more angry the alienating parent, the more anger expressed by their child towards the alienated parent. Most significant were the differences between the severe and mild groups of children.

The data were able to significantly differentiate the severe group of alienated children from the moderate and mild groups. The children in the severe group had more negative behaviors of PAS than did children in the moderate and mild groups. The moderate group of children had more negative behaviors than the mild group. The children in the moderate and severe groups may be at higher risk for problems in school and emotional problems such as depression. As the level of negative behaviors in children increase, so does the presence of PAS symptoms and its severity.

In this study, no children in the mild group expressed anger at the alienated parent, but 18 out of 20 expressed anger in the severe group. This is significant and may indicate the parent is expressing anger about the other parent which is accepted by and expressed by the child. Additionally, one child out of 22 children in the mild group refused visitation whereas 17 out of 20 children in the severe group refused visitation. The parents in the severe category had more negative behaviors. This indicates the more negative the parent's behaviors, the more negative the child's behavior. Consequently, the alienated parent's relationship with the child is disrupted.

The results of this study appear to support the existence of PAS. Children in the severe group present as more disturbed than children in the mild group.

More children in the severe group had fewer visitations, less affection, fewer positive feelings, more denigration, and more anger towards the alienated parent. These five (5) categories were summed to obtain a total number of symptoms observed in each child of each family. The children in the mild group had fewer negative behaviors than the moderate or severe PAS groups. In other words, the mild PAS children expressed more positive behaviors towards the alienated parent. The children in the severe group had more negative behaviors. The amount of negative behaviors and symptoms appears to be directly related to the amount of hostility exhibited by the alienating parent towards the alienated parent.

This vilification by the alienating parent is both covert and overt and in the presence of the child. For example, the alienating parent might express "fear" of the alienated parent in order to disrupt the parent-child relation. This fear is transferred to the child in a variety of contexts. Allegations of abuse, including molest, by the alienated parent are common. If these allegations appear after the parents separate, this may need very careful evaluation and also an investigation by the authorities. This may be a device to sever the parent-child relation.

Clinical observations and evaluation of the entire family, including contact with collateral sources may help reveal the all too familiar behaviors of PAS for both the parents and the children. Intensive investigation and observation of the children and family is necessary to help determine if PAS is present.

Researchers and clinicians still question why Gardner described PAS as a syndrome. Gardner considered PAS a syndrome because it is a "grouping of signs and symptoms that suggest a common underlying pathogenesis, course, familial pattern, or treatment selection" (DSM 4th.Ed., 1994). It is the goal of this study to determine whether PAS can be supported, not if it is a syndrome.

Observations of PAS made a very important contribution to the field of family law. It alerted the legal system that children's statements about rejecting one parent may be the result of both overt or covert manipulation by one parent. It gave clear and specific recommendations about a combination of legal and therapeutic interventions, the "most important of which was the need for a court order for continued contact between parent and child" (Lund, M. 1995). The findings from this study's 30 cases with 59 children does appear to support the existence of PAS.

The criticism and denial of PAS by practitioners is unjustified. The concept of PAS includes the brainwashing component, but is much more comprehensive. PAS refers to the alienating parent as "programming" the child against the alienated parent. PAS emphasizes the combination of the child's own scenarios of denigration of the alienated parent and the alienating parent's programming. PAS is Gardner's term which includes and encompasses both contributory factors from the child and alienating parent.

PAS is not animosity that a child harbors against a parent who has actually abused a child. PAS is never considered if the alienated parent is found neglectful and/or abusive. In such cases, it is appropriate for the child to want to resist contact with the abusing parent. "PAS is applicable only when the [alienated] parent has not exhibited anything close to the degree of alienating behavior that might warrant the campaign of denigration exhibited by the child" (Gardner, 1992, p. 64). Rather, in typical cases, the alienated parent would be considered by most practitioners to have been a normal, loving parent or at worst, exhibited minimal impairments in parenting capacity.

Moreover, the child is an active participant in PAS who wants to maintain the parent-child bond with the alienating parent. The child is psychologically bonded to both parents, but has a stronger psychological bond with the alienating parent.

The phenomenon of PAS occurs in the context of a highly conflicted family system which is composed of a child, alienating parent, and alienated parent who is victimized by this process. Actually, the child is the real victim in the end. This study indicates that the child becomes estranged from the alienated parent by the alienating parent. This family system has a number of identifiable signs, symptoms, and behaviors. The characteristics and behaviors of the alienating parents, the alienated parents, the children, as well as, the techniques used in this study appear to support observations of PAS.

Children are naïve, simplistic and unsophisticated and cannot provide themselves with credible and meaningful mechanisms to protect themselves against a parent who is determined to split the child's relationship with his/her other parent. Alienating parents welcome the child's expression of complaints about the alienated parent. These inconsequential complaints by children and their absurdity are the hallmark of the child's contribution to the development of PAS.

The child identifies with the alienating parent as PAS progresses and the alienated parent becomes viewed as loathsome. Deprived of the alienated parent for identification, the child may then switch to the alienating parent as the only parent to emulate. When the alienated parent criticizes the alienating parent, it is the same as criticizing the child in that child's mind. The child has become identified completely with the alienating parent in severe PAS. These children can become vigilant and highly attuned with the alienating parent. To disappoint or abandon the emotionally volatile, depressed, fragile, or raging [alienating] parent could result in punishment, rejection, or being ignored. The child acts as though the alienating parent's survival depends upon his or her caretaking (Johnston and Roseby, 1997).

Kopetski (1991) reported on 84 PAS cases from a sample of 413 court ordered custody evaluations in Colorado. Prior to learning of Gardner's work, Kopetski's team independently reached similar conclusions regarding parental alienation (PAS). Kopetski characterizes PAS as a form of psychosocial pathology in which a parent psychologically exploits the child and appropriates social systems in order to achieve alienation. In 18 percent of Kopetski's study, the alienating parent was successful in preventing the child from having a relationship with the alienated parent by denigrating the alienated parent and programming the child. The alienation was often supported by a therapist on the basis that the child should not be separated from a 'symbiotic relationship'. In other words, the therapist would collude with the child and support the child's position recommending the child not have contact with the alienated parent.

Descriptive statistics were used to describe this study's findings for the "presence" or "absence" of PAS. The data obtained from the thirty case sample describes parents using the parental criteria for PAS: mild, moderate and severe. Data from the criteria for children's symptoms with PAS: mild, moderate, and severe are reviewed for each case. Nonparametric statistics analyzed the difference between the children's groups, as well as, the demographic data obtained.

Children in the severe PAS group in this study are more disturbed than children in the moderate PAS group or children in the mild PAS group. The severe PAS children exhibit more negative behavioral symptoms towards the alienated parent. These children have disrupted parent-child relations with the alienated parent. This study found there were more children who were angry, denigrating, had fewer positive feelings, less expression of feelings and resisted visitation in the severe PAS category than in the children's mild group or children's moderate PAS group.

Conclusions

The data from this study appears to support Dr. Gardner's observations of PAS published in 1985. The data from this study indicates that parents in the mild PAS category have children who exhibit fewer negative behaviors towards the alienated parent. For example, there were 22 children in the mild anger group and no anger was expressed towards the alienated parent. Contrarily, in the severe anger group, 18 out of 20 children expressed anger towards the alienated parent and more of their parents were angry. In its severe form, PAS is more distinctive than the mild form. PAS is destructive to a child's relationship with the alienated parent. Severe PAS can be irreversible in its effects. Severe PAS is destructive irrespective of the gender of the alienating parent. Children's negative behaviors towards the alienating parent increase in severity as the negative behaviors and hostility of the alienating parent increases. The results of this data are significant.

Children with mild PAS exhibit fewer negative behaviors and typically maintain contact with the alienated parent; whereas, children in the severe PAS group are more resistant to contact with the alienated parent. The parent-child relations become very impaired with severe PAS. The hostility of the alienating parent never seems reasonably linked to the seriousness of the incidents alleged. The alienating parent insists upon viewing the alienated parent as all "negative" without the ability to see even potential positive traits of the alienated parent. Severely alienated children can see no "good" about the alienated parent. These severe children "split" their parents: the alienating parent is all good and the alienated parent is all bad. These contentions of rejecting the alienated parent begin to sound like the decision of the child. These children have an absence of guilt towards their once loved parent. This was all recognized by Gardner in 1985. PAS is probably just as prevalent in family law disputes today as it was in 1985, if not more prevalent. Also, this study supports the seriousness of PAS, particularly the moderate and severe types.

Whether one chooses to use PAS terminology or not, the serious problems posed by these intractable high conflict custody cases are very real. The behaviors observed in the severe cases manifest exactly as described by Gardner. An appropriate diagnosis, including level of severity is essential to stop the progression of PAS.

Recommendations

Continued research is needed. This study consists of a small number of cases; larger studies would allow for greater generalization. Further, research in related areas could include: 1) legal intervention depending on the severity of the PAS; 2) court ordered mental health treatment; 3) legal intervention to protect the children including court ordered case management, special master, minor's counsel or which ever combination works best depending on the severity of PAS; 4) court ordered Evidence Code 730 Evaluation of all family members; 5) re-measurement of the evaluation either clinically and/or by testing to determine if there has been improvement in the parent-child relations subsequent to the treatment; 6) psychological evaluation of the entire family prior to reversal of custody in severe cases and; 7) intervention for the children, including court intervention which may include a revised parenting plan, reversal of custody or third-party placement for the child pending family treatment; and 8) mental health treatment for the child by a senior therapist trained in high conflict custody cases.

Early recognition and intervention will minimize the effects of PAS and improve parent-child relations. The courts must become educated on PAS because false allegations of sexual/physical abuse are common. Law enforcement and Child Protective Services may become involved and actually become "brainwashed" by the alienating parent. This may also occur in the attorneys, family court services, and private counselors who become involved. The opinions of various professionals who become involved in PAS cases should not be accepted as authoritative simply because these are individuals designated as "professionals." Professionals' opinions must be tested and critically evaluated by the courts, their professional colleagues, and review committees. The collusion by other professionals with the alienating parent is one of the most common reasons for the perpetuation of PAS. Education of PAS and its effects on families engaged in custody disputes is greatly needed by the courts, law enforcement agencies, and mental health community.

APPENDICES

APPENDIX A

INITIAL INTAKE: PARENTAL INTERVIEW

1. History of relationship:

      1a.   Mother's version:

      1b.   Father's version:

2.   History of caregiving and parenting during their intact relationship:

3.   Father's role:

4.   Mother's role:

5.   Mother's concerns:

6.   Father's concerns:

7.   Current parenting schedule:

8.   Mother's goals and proposals for parenting:

9.   Father's goals and proposals for parenting:

10.   Cooperative parenting? Alignment? PAS?

11.   Symptomology noted:

Anger, Paranoia, Programming Minor, Willingness to share parenting with the other parent, Desire for vengeance, Believes other parent should be involved in child's life, Interferes with visitation, Complies with court orders, Allegations of sex/physical abuse.

APPENDIX B

INTERVIEW WITH MINOR CHILD

1.   Engagement phase of child, clarify my role, create empathy for child.

2.   Please tell me why you think you are here with me today?

3.   Has anyone told you what to say or do during your visit with me?

4.   What did Mom tell you? Dad? What does that mean? (listen for PAS, I view our conversation as confidential verses nonconfidential).

5.   Can you tell me a little bit about the school you attend?

6.   Can you tell me a little bit about your friends and what you enjoy doing with your friends?

7.   Did you see Mom and Dad fight? Hit anyone? Swear? Scream? You? Mom? Dad?

8.   Tell me about your family and the members of your family?

9.   What do you enjoy doing with your Mother? (Give feedback and protect privacy of the child.)

10. What do you enjoy doing with your Father? (Give feedback and protect privacy of the child.)

11. What do your enjoy doing with your brothers or sisters?

12. Can you tell me if you had one wish what that wish would be?

13. How has this been for you?

14. Why do you think this is going on?

15. How does this work for you?

16. Do you have any thoughts about what I can say to your parents?

17.   Observation of infants and parents are separate for each parent and child. Look for bonding, attachment, and care-giving ability.

APPENDIX C

Criteria for PAS, Children's Symptoms

Mild PAS									
Case No.	Child No.	Gender	Age	Race	Visitation w/AP	Expression of affection w/AP	Positive feelings about AP	Anger at AP	Denigration of AP

Moderate PAS									
Case No.	Child No.	Gender	Age	Race	Visitation w/AP	Denigration of AP	Express affection w/AP when alone	Anger at AP	Positive feelings about AP

Severe PAS								
Case No.	Child No.	Gender	Age	Race	Visitation strongly Resisted w/AP	Denigration of AP	Express affection w/AP when alone	Anger at AP	Positive feelings for AP

APPENDIX D

Criteria for PAS, Parents Symptoms

Mild PAS

Case No.	Gender	Age	Race	Desire for vengeance	Slight Programming of Child	Anger	Believes AP should be involved in child's life	Strong preference for Sole PPC	

Moderate PAS

Case No.	Gender	Age	Race	Paranoia	Programming Child	Interferes with visitation	Unreceptive to complying w/ Court orders	Anger	Allegations of sex/physical abuse

Severe PAS

Case No.	Gender	Age	Race	Paranoia	Anger	Programming the Child	Fanatic to Prevent/ interrupt visitation	False allegations sex/physical abuse	Unreceptive to complying w/ Court orders

APPENDIX E

Information Letter to Court Referred Cases

July 24, 2000

This is to inform you that I am conducting a study involving high conflict custody cases. Information and knowledge about family dynamics during custody disputes is sought. The purpose of this study is to expand the understanding of families who experience high conflict during custody disputes. Additionally, knowledge will be gained about the child's response to their parents' conflict.

This letter is to inform you of this study and that data from your records will be included. The procedure used will be review of court records and files. The confidentiality of these records and their contents will be maintained at all time. There will be no names, dates, locations, or any other identifying information cited. There is no compensation for use of this information.

You may call me to request that your records not be part of this study. Further, if you have questions about this study, please contact me by leaving a message on my confidential voicemail at (916) 485-7797.

The benefit gained from this study will be greater understanding of the dynamics of high conflict custody disputes and its effect upon the children.

All questions regarding this study will be answered. A copy of the final study will be made available to you upon request.

If you have any questions, you may call me at or leave a confidential voicemail message at (916-485-7797).

Thank you,

_____   _____
Janelle Burrill, J.D., LCSW   **Date**
Board Certified Diplomate

APPENDIX F

Ethics Committee Application

Application for Approval for the Use of Non-public Court Records

Researcher: Janelle Burrill-O'Donnell   July 4, 2000

Full Address: 1107 Sand Bar Circle, Carmichael, CA 95608

Phone(Day): (916) 646-6500 Phone(Eve): (916) 485-7797   Chair: Dr. Sumpter

Title of Activity: Ph.D. Dissertation: Parental Alienation Syndrome in Court Referred
Custody Cases

Sponsoring Organization: N/A   Contact Person: N/A

I will conduct the study identified in the attached application. If I decide to make any changes in the procedures or if any problems arise, I will immediately report such occurrences or contemplated changes to the Ethics Committee for their review and possible action.

Investigator Signature:_____   Date:_____

I have read and approve this protocol, and I believe that the investigator is competent to conduct the activity as described in the application.

Chair, Dissertation Committee: _____ Date:_____

The signature of the Chair of the Ethics Committee, when affixed below, indicates that the activity identified above and described in the attached pages has been approved.

Chair, Ethics Committee: _____   Date:_____

Ethics Committee Application cont.

1. Data: The data will be obtained from the Family Law Relations Court. The cases were intractable custody disputes referred for evaluation, mediation, or counseling. The thirty, court referred custody cases, not yet resolved will become part of this study.

2. Procedures: This study will use the case study method to identify the "presence" or "absence" of parental symptoms using the criteria for Parental Alienation Syndrome (PAS). The children's data from each case will be compared and reviewed according to PAS children's criteria for mild, moderate, and severe. Each case will be reviewed to determine whether it meets the criteria of PAS. The children's groups will be reviewed to determine if there is a difference in the three groups of children based on their behaviors and symptoms. Because the variables of interest are dichotomous in nature ("present" vs. "absent"), descriptive statistics will be used to verify the presence or absence of PAS. Demographics will be reviewed and compared.

Information about this study will be mailed to each person whose file will be included in this study. Each person whose record is reviewed will be notified that data from their records will be included in this study. Confidentiality will be respected and maintained.

3. Information Letter: The attached copy of the information letter about this study will be sent to individuals whose records will be included in this study. Confidentiality will be maintained.

4. Safeguards: To minimize any potential to breach of confidentiality, only this researcher will have access to any identifying information in this study. No one, including support staff will have access to identifying data contained in the files. This should avoid any potential for breach of confidentiality.

5. Benefits: Support of Parental Alienation Syndrome will result in greater acceptance in the legal and mental health communities benefiting children's emotional well-being and their parent-child relations. Increased acceptance and identification of PAS will improve diagnosis and treatment to avoid further harm to children and their parent-child relationships.

6. Post Experiment Interview: Notification of completion of this study will mailed to those whose data was used in the study.

7. Attachments: Informational Letter to the individuals whose files and data will be used in this study.

REFERENCES

1. American Psychiatric Association (1994). Diagnostic and statistical manual of mental disorders (4th Ed.). Washington, D.C.: Author.

2. Anastasi, A, Urbina, S. (1997). Psychological testing, 7th Ed. Prentice Hall: NJ.

3. Bee, H. (1985). The developing child: NY: Harper & Row.

4. Berk, L. (1997). Child development, 4thEd., Allyn & Bacon: Boston.

5. Blush, G., Ross, K (1987). Sexual allegation in divorce: the SAID syndrome. Conciliation courts review, vol. 25(1), 1-11.

6. Calabrese, R., Miller, J., Dooley, B. (1987). The identification of alienated parents and children: Implications for school psychologists. Psychology in the schools. Vol. 24(2) 145-150.

7. Campbell, K., (1982). The psychotherapy relationship for borderline personality disorders: Psychotherapy: research and practice, 19 (2). (pp.166-86).

8. Caplan, F., Caplan, T. (1980). The second twelve months of life: your baby's growth month by month Bantam: NY.

9. Cartwright, G. (1993). Expanding the parameters of parental alienation syndrome. American Journal of Family Therapy. Vol. 21(3), 205-215.

10. Craig, R. (1997). Clinical and diagnostic interviewing. Jason Aronson: NJ.

11. Doherty, W., Kouneski, E, & Erickson, M. Responsible fathering: and overview and conceptual framework. University of Minnesota, September 1997.

12. Donaldson-Pressman, S. & Pressman, R. (1994). The narcissistic family, diagnosis, and treatment. New York: Lexington.

13. Dunne, J., Hedrick, M. (1994). The parental alienation syndrome: analysis of sixteen selected cases. Journal of Divorce & Remarriage. Vol. 21 3-4), 21-38.

14. Evergreen Consultants in Human Behavior (1997). What is attachment disorder? Axces.Com.

15. F. Turner (1988). Child psychopathology: a social work perspective. New York: Freepress.

16. Faller, K. (1998). The parental alienation syndrome. What is it and what data support it? Child maltreatment: journal of the american professional society on the abuse of children, May vol. 3(2), 100-115.

17. Folberg, J., Milne, A. (1988). Divorce mediation. New York: Gilford Press.

18. Folberg, J. (1991). Joint custody and shared parenting. New York: Gilford Press.

19. Gardner, R. (1984). Recommendations for dealing with parents who induce a parental alienation syndrome in their children, a guide for mental health and legal professionals. Cresskill, NJ: Creative Therapeutics.

20. Gardner, R. (1986). Child custody litigation. Creskill, NJ: Creative Therapeutics.

21. Gardner, R. (1986). Family evaluation and child custody mediation, arbitration, and litigation. Cresskill, NJ: Creative Therapeutics.

22. Gardner, R. (1986). The psychotherapeutic techniques of Richard A. Gardner. Rev. ed., Cresskill, NJ: Creative Therapeutics.

23. Gardner, R. (1991). Sex abuse hysteria. Cresskill, NJ: Creative Therapeutics.

24. Gardner, R. (1992). The parental alienation syndrome. Cresskill, NJ: Creative Therapeutics.

25. Gardner. R. (1992) The parents book about divorce. (Rev. ed.) New York: Bantam.

26. Gardner, R. (1998). The parental alienation syndrome: what is it and what data support it? Comment. Child maltreatment: journal of the american professional society on the abuse of children vol. 3(4) 309-312.

27. Gardner, R. (1998). Recommendations for dealing with parents who induce a parental alienation syndrome in their children. Journal of divorce and remarriage, vol. 28(3-4) 1-28.

28. Gardner, R. (1999). Differentiating between parental alienation syndrome and bona fide abuse-neglect. American journal of family therapy, Apr-Jun vol. 27(2), 97-107.

29. Gardner, R. (1999). Family therapy of the moderate type of parental alienation syndrome. American journal of family therapy, vol. 27(3) 195-212.

30. Gardner, R., A., (1989). Family evaluation in child custody mediation, arbitration, and litigation. Cresskill, NJ: Creative Therapeutics.

31. Gardner, R. (1987). The Parental alienation syndrome and the differentiation between fabricated and genuine child sex abuse. Cresskill, NJ: Creative Therapeutics.

32. Geffner, R. (1992). Guidelines for using mediation with abusive couples. Psychotherapy in private practice, vol. 10(1-2) 77-92.

33. Greenspan, S. (1990). The development of the ego. Madison, CT: International Universities Press, Inc., (1994). Guidelines for child custody evaluations in divorce proceedings. American Psychological Association.

34. Heinz, M., Grisso, T. (1996). Review of instruments assessing parenting competencies used in child custody evaluations. Behavioral sciences and the law, vol. 14(3), 293-313.

35. Hilsenroth, M., Hibbard, S., Nash, M., Handler, L., (1993). A research study of narcissism, defense, and aggression in borderline, narcissistic and Cluster C personality disorders. Journal of personality assessment, Apr., vol. 60, 346-361.

36. Huntington, D., S., (1986). The forgotten figures in divorce and fatherhood: The Struggle for Parental Identity. Edited by Jacobs, J., W., Washington DC, American Psychiatric Association Press.

37. Hysjulien, C., Wood, B., Benjamin, G., Andrew, H. (1994). Child custody evaluations: A review of methods used in litigation and alternative dispute resolution. Family & conciliation courts review vol. 32(4). 466-489.

38. Johnson, J., Roseby, V. (1997). In the name of the child: A developmental approach to understanding and helping children of conflicted and violent divorce. NY: The Free Press.

39. Johnston, J., & Campbell, L. (1988). Impasses of divorce. New York: The Free Press.

40. Johnston, J., R., (1993). Children of divorce who refuse visitation, in nonresidential parenting: new vistas in family living. Edited by Depner, CE., Bray JH, London, Sage Publications.

41. Kelley, J. (1996) Divorce related distortions in parent-child relationships: parental alignment and alienation. Unpublished.

42. Kernberg, O. (1986). Severe personality disorders. CT: Yale University Press.

43. Kreisman, J., Straus. H. (1989). I hate you, don't leave me. CA: The Body Press.

44. Lampel, A. (1999). Use of the Million Clinical Multiaxial Inventory-III in evaluating child custody litigants. American journal of forensic psychology, vol.17(4), 19-31.

45. Livesley, W. (1995) DSM IV personality disorders. New York: Gilford Press.

46. Lowenstein, L. (1998). Parental alienation syndrome: a two-step approach toward a solution. Contemporary family therapy: an international journal, Dec. vol. 20(4), 505-520.

47. Lund, M. (1995). A therapist's view of parental alienation syndrome. Family and conciliation courts review, July vol. 33 (3), 308-316.

48. M. Ehrenber, Hunter, M., Elterman, M. (1996). Shared parenting agreements after marital separation: the roles of empathy and narcissism. Journal of consulting and clinical psychology, vol. 64 (4), 808-818.

49. Maccoby, E., Buchanan, C., Mnookin, R., Dornbusch, S., (1993). Post divorce roles of mothers and fathers in the lives of their children. Journal of family psychology, vol. 7(1), 24-38.

50. Manfield, P. (1992). Split self/split object. NJ: Jason Aronson, Inc.

51. Millon, T. (1981). Disorders of personality DSM III: Axis II. New York: John Wiley & Sons.

52. National Center on Child Abuse and Neglect, Executive Summary (1988). Study of national incidence and prevalence of child abuse and neglect. Washington, D.C.: Department of Health and Human Services, Contract 105-85-1702.

53. National Council on Children's Rights: CAPTA revised to provide relief for false allegations. speak out for children, Fall 1996/Winter 1997.

54. Nicholas, L. (1995). Parental alienation: assessing and treating coercion of children during divorce and custody disputes. Unpublished, Sacramento, CA.

55. Nicholas, L. (1997). Does parental alienation exist? A preliminary empirical study of the phenomenon in custody and visitation disputes? Unpublished, Sacramento, CA, Private Mediators.

56. Nurcombe, B., Partlett, D. (1994). Child mental health and the law. New York: Freepress.

57. Othmer, E., & Othmer, S. (1994). The clinical interview using DSM IV, Volume I: fundamentals. Washington, DC: American Psychiatric Press.

59. Palmer, N. (1988). Legal recognition of the parental alienation syndrome. American journal of family therapy, vol. 16(4), 361-363.

60. Pett, M., Wampold, B., Turner, C., Vaughan-Cole, B., (1999). Paths of influence of divorce on preschool children's psychosocial adjustment. Journal of family psychology, vol. 13(2), 145-64.

61. Rand, D. (1997). The spectrum of parental alienation syndrome (part I, II). American journal of forensic psychology vol. 15(4), 39-92.

62. Rosen, K., Rothbaum, F. (1993). Quality of parental caregiving and security of attachment. Developmental psychology, Mar., vol. 29, No. 2, 358-367.

63. Siegel, J. (1996). Traditional MMPI-2 validity indicators and initial presentation in custody evaluation. American journal of forensic psychology vol. 14(3), 55-63.

64. Siegel, J., Langford, J. (1998). MMPI-2 validity scales and suspected parental alienation syndrome. American journal of forensic psychology, vol. 16(4), 5-14.

65. Simon, L. (1995). A therapeutic jurisprudence approach to the legal processing of domestic violence cases. Psychology, public policy and law, vol. 1(1), 43-79.

66. Singer, D. (1993). Playing for their lives. New York: Free Press.

67. Stahl, P. (1994). Conducting child custody evaluations. CA: Sage Press.

68. Stahl, P. Alienation and alignment of children. California Psychologist March 1999.

69. Stahl, P. (1999). Complex issues in child custody evaluations. CA: Sage Press.

70. Sullivan, M., (2000). The alienated child, presented at the Sacramento Valley Psychological Association annual seminar.

71. Turkat, I. (1994). Child visitation interference in divorce. Clinical psychology review, vol. 14(8), 737-742.

72. Vestal, A. (1999). Mediation and parental alienation syndrome. Family & conciliation courts review, vol.37(4), 487-503.

73. Wallerstein, J., & Kelly, J. (1980). Surviving the breakup. CA: Basic Books.

74. Wallerstein J., S., Blakeslee, S. (1989). Second Chances. New York: Tricknor & Fields.

75. Warshak, R. (1992). The custody revolution. New York: Poseidon Press.

Printed in the United States
104208LV00007B/13/A

9 781581 121490